Erma Bombeck

I WANT TO GROW HAIR,

I WANT TO GROW UP,

I WANT TO GO TO BOISE

CHILDREN SURVIVING CANCER

Harper Paperbacks

Harper & Row, Publishers, New York
Grand Rapids, Philadelphia, St. Louis, San Francisco
London, Singapore, Sydney, Tokyo, Toronto

Harper Paperbacks a division of Harper & Row, Publishers, Inc.
10 East 53rd Street, New York, N.Y. 10022

A hardcover edition of this book was published in
1989 by Harper & Row, Publishers, Inc.

Cover art by Hal Just
Book design by Karen Savary

First Harper Paperbacks printing: September 1990

Printed in the United States of America

HARPER PAPERBACKS and colophon are trademarks
of Harper & Row, Publishers, Inc.

10 9 8 7 6 5 4 3 2 1

IF I AM THE MOTHER OF THIS BOOK,
THEN ANN WHEAT IS ITS MIDWIFE . . .
AND THESE ARE ITS CHILDREN.

Publisher's Note

All monies earned by the author from
sales of this book in the United States will
go to the research division of the
American Cancer Society.

All monies earned by the author from
sales of this book in Canada will go to the
Canadian Cancer Society.

All monies earned by the author from
sales of this book outside the United
States and Canada will go to the Eleanor
Roosevelt International Cancer Research
Fellowships.

Contents

Introduction

Whenever I told someone I was writing a new book, they would break into a smile and ask, "What's it about this time?"

When I said it was a book on children surviving cancer, the expression on their faces changed. Their eyes took on a look of pain. Their smiles disappeared and their lips formed a firm line. They looked at me with a pity usually reserved for a woman who had just lost her bank card. When I explained that it would reflect humor and optimism, the look changed again—this time to one usually reserved for a woman who had just lost her mind.

Cancer and optimism were not considered compatible on this planet.

It occurred to me that this is what the children in this book see every time someone looks at them. At the moment they stop being a kid and turn into a child with cancer, the smiles disappear. Every face around them reflects a mixture of sadness, shock, pity or—worse—reverence for someone chosen to suffer.

Okay, to be honest, I had some misgivings myself at first when Ann Wheat, a young, energetic camp director from Camp Sunrise in Arizona, invited me to lunch to discuss a "project." "Kids with cancer need a little booklet or a pamphlet—something to give them a shot of optimism," she said. "Not every kid who has cancer dies, and they need to know that. They are isolated by the disease and its treatment. You cannot imagine how important it is for them to hear the voices of classmates, siblings, grandparents, doctors, counselors, teachers, friends, and parents who share their nightmare.

"You can do something upbeat," she pressed. "I know you can. Why, I'll bet you didn't know that teens have a contest to see who can wait the longest to throw up during chemo."

Be still, my beating heart! Was this the humor on which I was to feed? Without speaking, I summoned the waitress for the check!

Ann fired her final shot. "Look, there are anywhere from forty to ninety percent of kids out there with cancer who are surviving it. They deserve to be counted and they deserve a chance to live their lives as normally as is possible."

She was right. I could gather a few statistics, talk to some people, and pull together a little booklet in a matter of months.

On a Wednesday morning in July 1987, I flew

to Camp Sunrise, just outside of Payson, Arizona, to get acquainted with my material. It was your basic camp with musty tents and mosquitoes that should have been required to file flight plans.

The ultimate goals of these campers were not unlike the ultimate goals of campers everywhere: (1) to use food for the purpose for which it was meant to be used—fights; (2) to go home with the coveted Dry Soap award; and (3) to sock it to the staff. The last is deftly accomplished through a sixty-piece kazoo band at midnight, hanging a nurse's bicycle from the diving board, and planting things in the counselors' beds that crawl in the night causing them to hyperventilate.

But the differences in this camp were not exactly subtle. Artificial limbs and a wheelchair were stored in the corner of the lodge. Several of the campers were bald. A counselor with one leg told me how she visited a border town in Mexico that had had a rash of car-stripping incidents. So she took off her prosthesis and propped it up with the foot showing above the window ledge of the van so someone would think the car was occupied. Not your basic crime fighter, but it worked.

But there was another ritual that pointed out how unique these campers are. It happened around three in the afternoon when little kids with holes in the knees of their jeans and sagging socks climbed down from the trees, came down paths from their hikes, and abandoned their places on bases of the ball diamond. They headed for a small room with a handmade sign that read "MED SHED."

Sandra Priebe, who describes herself as a "gofer" at Camp Sunrise, had observed the ritual for several summers. "No one has to call them," she said. "They know. It's med time. They push open the door and leave their childhood behind them.

"As Sean takes his seat at the card table, his eyes lose the impishness and flash with the alertness that one would expect in an eagle. His ten-year-old size conflicts with his technical expertise. He has the ability to scan blood reports with the same rapid comprehension that his peers might scan comic books.

"When his plastic tray is presented to him, he explains to the nurse the procedure while she listens intently. Each tray is a parent's hope; a child's future. The lines are flushed, and proper swabbing is complete. He leaves the shed to resume his civilian job of dirt wallower, teaser of girls, and climber of trees."

When the late afternoon rains came, I joined a group of ten teenagers jammed in a small, parked RV that normally would have accommodated a little retired couple seeing America first. It was the hour set aside at camp to explore and share feelings.

I edged my way past a pretty nineteen-year-old girl perched on a counter with half of her body in the sink. A boy was sprawled out on the bed staring at the ceiling. The rest of us found seats around the small table. Mercifully, someone cracked a window.

As they talked, I saw and heard their uniqueness. Here was a group of children who had been poked at, x-rayed, smothered with love, ridiculed, punctured, spoiled, abandoned by friends, pitied, counseled, experimented with, lied to, protected, resented, and stared at. They had rarely been listened to.

They were children who had been robbed of their innocence and their childhood, neither of which they would ever recapture again.

They were children who had been sentenced to a period of uncertainty and pain usually inflicted on the elderly who had lived rich, long lives. They were little people whom destiny had tapped on the shoulder and announced, "We interrupt this life to bring you a message of horror."

I expected to hear anger about the disease that brought all of them to this airless trailer on a July afternoon. I didn't hear it.

I expected despair over the hand of cards they had been dealt. That didn't happen either.

I expected fear of a future that held no warranties—no guarantees. It never came up.

What they did talk about were the people who don't appreciate each day. One eighteen-year-old talked about his friends on drugs. He told them, "You wanna do drugs? Do chemo for a year. It'll give you the same effect and make you feel just as lousy."

They talked about how wonderful it would be if people would let them get on with their lives. "We need hate once in awhile," said one. "I had a teacher last year who shouted at me on the first day of school, 'Sit down and be quiet!' She treated me like everyone else. I knew it was going to be a good year."

"Yeah," said a sixteen-year-old boy. "It's like people whisper around you and they never laugh. Man, without a sense of humor I wouldn't have made it this far."

As they talked and laughed about their lives, suddenly I felt like I was the innocent child and they were the adults, dispensing wisdom. And I knew then these kids deserved better than buckets of tears and public pity. Their legacy was too important to pack away like a fading photograph. In a world short on role models, they set standards that can never be topped.

They tested drugs and served as experimental pincushions in the war to eradicate one of the most devastating diseases of this century. Without them, this book on cancer survival could never have been considered.

The survival rates tabulated in 1989 by St. Jude Children's Research Hospital in Memphis could serve as a national monument to their courage.

Since 1962, the survival of acute lymphocytic leukemia up from 0 to 60 percent . . . Ewing's sarcoma
up from 5 to 60 percent . . . non-Hodgkin's lymphoma from 6 to 80 percent . . . Hodgkin's disease
from 50 to 90 percent . . . retinoblastoma from 75
to 90 percent . . . Wilms' tumor from 50 percent to
90 percent . . . osteosarcoma from 20 to 60 percent.

But, more important, their very being gives us
a real sense of what this life is all about if we listen.

The hopelessness I had brought in with me
dissipated.

The answer was somewhere within these ten
kids. They seemed to have come to terms with their
common enemy and were prepared to give it the
fight of their lives. I couldn't pity them. Pity is
reserved for those who have no fight left in them.

They reminded me of candles in the wind who
accept the possibility that at best they are in danger
of being extinguished by a gust of wind from no-
where and yet, as they flicker and dance to remain
alive, their brilliance challenges the darkness and
dazzles those of us who watch their light.

The rain had stopped as we shuffled out the
door. Two of the last ones to leave the trailer were
Sandy and Anna. Sandy was the facilitator of the
group, the one with half her body in the sink. She
has Hodgkin's disease.

Her friend, Anna, just graduated from high
school. A khaki fatigue hat balanced atop her head.

Her radiance belied the fact that she is under treatment for leukemia.

The two joined arms and sloshed through the mud together as they shared a private joke. They looked to me to make sure I heard it. "So, you come here often?" asked Sandy. "What's your sign?"

Anna giggled, "Cancer, of course."

Both looked to me for a reaction and got one. They were outrageous and they knew it.

On the way home I wondered if an optimistic book on cancer were possible. Did I dare divest these young people of their pedestals? They aren't saints endowed with a special gift. They are children fighting a disease some of them can't even spell. Could I defend their dark humor at the risk of offending people? Was it possible to write a book about life where death sometimes writes the ending?

Where would I gather the material for it, other than camps and stories in the Candlelighters' publication? (The Candlelighters is a grass roots organization that offers support to families of children with cancer.)

In the weeks that followed, news of the proposed book spread. The first wave of what was to become hundreds of letters began to cover my desk. One mother wrote, "Humor is what got all of us through the clinic visits, the hospital stays, the blood tests, the loss of hair and weight. There is always something on the light side if you look for it. I'm sure people think, 'How can he laugh when he has cancer?' Our human nature is such that we can't feel terribly bad all the time."

Another letter from a seventeen-year-old boy said, "Face it. You've got to be like me to really appreciate how silly it is to read a letter in Dear Abby's column about a woman upset because her neighbor hasn't returned her salad bowls. It's like, "Ooooh lady, how can you stand it?" One of my philosophies is that you know it's happening, so you might as well laugh with it. If I were serious about this situation all the time, I'd be crying all the time. Who wants that?"

As the summer gave way to fall, the responses, from every state in the union and from Canada, France, and New Zealand, filled my dining room table and spilled over into cardboard boxes.

I made my decision. Humor and optimism had kept these kids in the mainstream of life. Perhaps laughing and believing in themselves was a major part of their survival. These were kids who had every intention of living long enough to go to Disneyland, drive their mothers crazy, live in bedrooms that should be condemned, go to the prom, eat pizza for breakfast, and grow old.

I was looking at a book of triumph—maybe not over the disease but over despair. Not only the kids, but everyone who had been touched by cancer had to come to terms with it—the exhausted, guilt-ridden mother, the father who lost his five-year-old child, the sibling who felt abandoned, the camp counselor who couldn't stop crying, the nurses and doctors who were all cried out, the friends who wanted to help but didn't know how.

When the first three chapters of my original manuscript were read around a campfire to see if the children approved of the way "their" book was going, there was silence at first. Then they said politely they liked it, but added, "You just gotta make it funnier."

"Right," I said, jotting "funnier" down on a yellow tablet.

"And the first chapter is all wrong," they said.

"What do you mean it's all wrong?"

They spoke with one voice. "The first chapter should be 'Am I Gonna Die?' because that's what everyone thinks about when they're first diagnosed."

Somehow I knew when I finished this book, I would never be the same person I was when I started it.

1

"Am I Gonna Die?"

"My mother said, 'You're not going to die.' "
"Did you believe her?"
"Hey, when my mother says something you
  don't dare question it."

Ann, age 10
Page, Arizona

This has to be a test.

Not only can I not begin to "make it funnier" with a chapter called "Am I Gonna Die?" but I have the added frustration of everyone thinking I'm writing a book on children with Terminal Cancer. I am writing a book on children with a disease called cancer who, with every day they live, have a better chance of surviving it.

The two words—"Terminal Cancer"—have traveled in tandem for so long, people think they're married to one another. Well, it's time they split. As one doctor put it, "We're all terminal. Only cancer patients suffer from Terminal Cancer. Do heart patients suffer from Terminal Heart Pain or diabetics from Terminal Diabetes? Only cancer has the stigma. It's been criminalized. Besides, only death is inevitable." (With the possible exceptions of Santa Claus and Dick Clark, I would agree.)

If you should run across the word "terminal" anywhere beyond this chapter, be assured it will refer to a bus station or an airport.

"Am I gonna die?" Unless you have God's unlisted phone number in your Rolodex, who knows. Kids who were given lousy odds are still living . . . some who had good chances aren't.

There's been an abundance of books written about children who die in the last chapter. I've read most of them and they're beautiful and heart-wrenching tributes to their courage. But there are thousands of kids with cancer out there who are alive and who recover to live productive lives. We not only need to know they're there, we need to know what got them there.

The question of "odds" inevitably comes up. The problem is you can't count on 'em. If people believed in odds, who would have predicted that

Barbie would be unmarried at age thirty and ride around with Ken in that same stupid cardboard car he had in the sixties.

Doctors especially don't like to quote odds. It's like the kids say: "My doctor's favorite plant is the hedge." They usually say something like there are no such things as chances when you're talking about a child. It either works or it doesn't. There's no such thing as 50 percent or 60 percent or 20 percent. There's either 100 percent or zero. Naturally, they're going for the 100 percent—not the zero.

In nonmedical terms that children can relate to, surviving cancer in the eighties has a lot better odds than having your mother believe you're "doing nothing" when you're locked in the bathroom with the water running and the dog is tunneling under the door.

And they're infinitely higher than a teacher canceling an exam you've studied for.

If you dug up an old medical book from the sixties, it would tell you that childhood leukemia is incurable. The information is not only depressing, it's wrong. You shouldn't read any book on cancer that is older than five years. The progress has been that dramatic.

Most of the books quote Las Vegas odds anyway. They're the ones where the only way you can leave Vegas a winner is when, the moment you get off the plane, you walk right into the propeller. Cancer odds are not that way anymore.

The tide of the battle turned in 1973. It was a big year for cancer patients. They didn't find a cure. But what they did find were different kinds of drugs in different combinations and better supportive therapy to get youngsters through the side effects of the drugs.

"Am I gonna die?" The question comes in many forms. Sometimes it's unspoken, but it's there. Sometimes the kids are real "cool" about it, like "I figured I will or I won't." Sometimes they are protective of their parents and insist they leave the room so they can discuss the question with their doctors like it is some kind of a sorority secret. Then they ask questions like "Is there a McDonald's in heaven?" and "Will I see my Grandpa who died two years ago?"

But what keeps surfacing throughout all the letters and interviews is the word "attitude." How important is it to the survival of a patient?

I couldn't find anyone who would rank it right up there with chemotherapy. Some pointed out that a great attitude is not always rewarded. They give it all they've got and they still lose. But a couple of doctors I talked with conceded that although it can't cure cancer, they see some pretty impressive results from being positive. The kids who flat out accept the disease on its terms don't seem to lose as much weight, miss as much school, and aren't in the hospital with infections in between treatments.

Others who are severely depressed throw up more, lose more weight, don't eat well, and don't bounce back as quickly.

Attitude is contagious and, in a family, can be crucial. Kids tend to take their cues from the people around them and handle it accordingly. Better to have a case of out-of-control optimism than to sentence the family to the Temple of Doom.

Several years ago there was a movie called *Chariots of Fire.* It was the story of a runner, Harold Abrahams, who was a member of the 1920 British Olympic team. After Harold lost a race to his archrival, he felt sorry for himself and said stubbornly to his girlfriend, "If I can't win, I won't run." She answered flatly, "If you don't run, you can't win."

"But," he whined, "I've worked so hard, what will I aim for?" She said quietly, "Beat him the next time."

One of the easiest tasks of writing this book was finding youngsters with cancer who had made up their minds to "run and win." They took personal pride in the fact that they were fighting something bigger than they were and stronger than they were . . . something that might even overpower them. But they still had something their enemy couldn't take away—hope. It's a formidable weapon.

When people are hovering over you looking

serious and worried, it is normal to question your future. Most of the children in this book asked "Am I gonna die?" and many of them got the answers they were looking for.

Maybe one of them was the teenager who rented you a boat last summer in Crestline, California. Maybe one of them was the married "thirtysomething" who taught your son at a school outside Chicago. Or if you dropped into a bank in Lebanon, Tennessee, perhaps the teller who took care of you was a small, pretty blond who also questioned her future. They are all survivors of cancer who discovered that when all else fails—pull out the big artillery, HOPE, and hang on!

2

"Have a Good Day"

An adult friend asked Christina what she would like for her eighth birthday. The small child, diagnosed with neuroblastoma, rubbed her hand over her bald head, then rested her face in her hands and said, "I don't know. I have two sticker books and a Cabbage Patch doll. I have everything."

Christina, age 12
Alpena, Michigan

This is a warning. If you can't handle optimism, don't go around children with cancer. If you feel tears are more appropriate than laughter, don't even think of dropping in on a camp where they are. If you don't want to put yourself at risk for feeling good about yourself, your life and the world . . . wear a mask!

Children of cancer are carriers of courage. There, you have been warned. Hang out with them and you will undergo a metamorphosis that you cannot control. You'll find yourself saying things like "Have a good day!" or "See you next year." I interviewed a scientist for this book and got so carried away I said, "What are you going to cure after you've found a cure for cancer?" and he replied without missing a beat, "Alzheimer's disease."

I visited a day camp in Phoenix one afternoon, and as I sat on a small chair with my knees under my chin, a small camper about three years old put his arm around my shoulder and positioned his face two inches from mine. "Do you know what?" he asked.

"What?" I answered back.

"I'm going to the circus this afternoon," he bubbled.

"That's wonderful," I gushed.

A counselor leaned over and said, "You're not going to the circus, Kenny. That's the other group. You're going swimming."

Most kids would have ripped out a sink and thrown it against the wall in disappointment. Instead, he turned to me and said with equal enthusiasm, "Do you know what?"

"What?" I asked.

"I'm going swimming this afternoon!"

Kenny would have gone to an opening of a can of tennis balls and been just as happy.

Kids with cancer seem to have a gift for cutting through the "what if," "what should've been," "what might have been," and getting right to "what is now." Bert was five years old and fighting neuroblastoma. He loved to draw. One day when he was asked, "Are you going to be an artist when you grow up?" he said indignantly, "I *am* an artist."

Or how about this insight from a child: "What good does it do if they cure the body but the person inside dies?"

If you don't believe optimism is contagious, there's the leukemia patient from Rhode Island, who was bumped from his flight at the airport. "But I have cancer," he said, "and would really like to get where I'm going tonight."

A man who overheard the conversation sprang from his seat in the crowd and said, "You can have my ticket, son." (As it turned out, the man didn't have a ticket either, but he meant well.)

And there was Frankie on his way home from his last day of chemotherapy in Philadelphia. He and his mother stopped at a restaurant to celebrate. The owner, noticing his baldness and guessing the rest, said the treat was on him.

Pity? A possibility. But I like to think there's a feeling that they are seeing courage face to face and want to be a part of it, no matter how small.

I was struck by the optimism of a mother from

Benson, Arizona, whose three-year-old daughter, Darlene, was diagnosed as having astrocytoma, a brain stem tumor.

To a mother who was trying to raise six children alone, the diagnosis could have triggered a falling apart scenario. But the whole family swung into action to alleviate the three-year-old's fears of the dark . . . and radiation:

"At night, we'd wrap Darlene in a white sheet and lay her on the kitchen table. Then we'd turn on the microwave for sound, turn off the lights so it would be dark, and put the portable sewing machine lid over her head and thump it with our fingers.

"We set the timer for thirty seconds at first and if she didn't move, then each time we did this we'd do it a little longer."

She also involved Darlene's brother and sisters in her full recovery: "I'd take one of them to Darlene's appointment and we'd stay the night at Ronald McDonald House and get the child a gift, showing them Darlene was not the only precious child in our home. Sometimes we'd drive to the mountains and look for pine cones and Darlene could hold the bag. We'd take the phone off the hook, shut the curtains, and just talk and laugh or feed the ducks on the lake." Darlene started school last year.

I was dazzled by the optimism of six-year-old Ryan of New River, Arizona, who was standing in a crowd of kids at a balloon race where a raffle for toys was in progress. Ryan stood there for over an hour with his ticket held tightly between his thumb and his forefinger.

As the crowd dispersed, Ryan walked over to the woman in charge and said quietly, "Would you call this number now?"

Jessica Hopkins of Sun Valley, Idaho, was nineteen when she was diagnosed as having leukemia. She was the number one singles player on the tennis team, and a month from graduation with a "great date" for the prom. Yet, she had something to prove. "Cancer had no place within me." Her priorities changed. "My number one goal was to get well again, not if my nails were painted. My life and the people's lives around me were completely rearranged overnight. School, tennis, and work were always first, but now I was first. I had endless hours to knit and sew, read and write, and best of all, sit and think. I viewed it as a chunk of the 'Recovery Process.'"

Today, Jessica is attending the University of Puget Sound—not your average freshman with her hat and pill jar collection and frequently bandage-covered hands, but "Who wants to be average anyway?

"I wish everyone who has cancer could benefit from it somehow," she wrote. "The saddest thing to me is when a person suffers through chemotherapy, radiation, and surgery and doesn't learn anything about themselves through the process. My cancer is a gift."

Sometimes, with these kids rattling around in an adult world of emotions, dangers, and decisions, you have to keep reminding yourself that they are children first. Inside these little bodies that house a full-blown major catastrophic disease are children fighting to get out. And children exist on a diet of optimism: The rain is always going to stop just before the Little League game begins. The lost library book will always turn up just before it is due. An Act of God will close the school when the term paper isn't finished.

Who but a child with cancer would list the following priorities?: "My three wishes are to (1) grow hair, (2) grow up, and (3) go to Boise." On the other hand, maybe the kid knows something about Boise no one else knows.

A father told a story about his daughter who lost a leg to Ewing's sarcoma. One night, very late, a young orderly came to her hospital room with a wheelchair to take her to x-ray. Her face was ashen, her eyelids at half-mast. She had her legs crossed and her one remaining foot was sticking out. The orderly put her in the wheelchair, put down the flaps, and positioned her one foot. Then he began to grope for the other one she didn't have. Finally, she looked at him and smiled. "Good luck!"

Optimism. If treated properly, it can only get better. Ask Melissa Denney. It kept her going . . . for eleven years.

3

Coming Home

> *"Mom was wheeling me in a wheelchair through Penney's at Christmas when Santa Claus came running over and said, 'Hello, little girl, what do you want for Christmas?' I said, 'I want a bicycle.' "*
>
> Melissa Denney
> Watertown, Tennessee

Melissa Denney, her mother Judy, and I literally toured the campus of Vanderbilt University in Nashville, Tennessee, in search of the "right" bench to conduct the interview. One was "too sunny," one was "too shady," one "too close to the street," and one was in the "sprinkler danger zone." You'd have thought we were going to buy it!

Finally, we hit pay dirt. I was sorry the interview couldn't have taken place in Melissa's home in Lebanon a few miles out of Nashville. I told her so. People are always more relaxed, more comfortable in homelike surroundings.

Melissa smiled as she took in the university's beautiful grounds harbored under a canopy of trees. "This is my home," she said. For eleven years she and her mother had come here in search of a cure for her cancer. "All the doctors and nurses and my friends are here. They're my family. Even though I'm cured, I still come back here once a year to see them. Some of the nurses are gone, but my doctors are still here. Some things don't change."

Perhaps the most dramatic change is Melissa herself. She was ten years old when she and her mother made their first trip to the Vanderbilt campus on a crisp October morning in 1977. As she checked into the hospital for tests, she was a little girl, pale, thin, feverish, scared, and so tired she could barely put one foot in front of the other.

On this day she was the picture of health in a pair of faded jeans and a knit shirt. We were barely settled when she opened the mysterious brown sack she had with her and pulled out a huge packet of photographs. "Let's see, I had them in some kind of order," she said, "but they've gotten mixed up. This is when I was first diagnosed and this was where I lost my hair the first time."

I watched the twenty-one-year-old as she excitedly extracted one picture after the other: her friends, "one normal, one bald, one swollen as big as a pig from prednisone" (a hormone that kills lymphocytes); her brother, Chuck, "He's twenty-five now and fixin' to get married"; and "Look at this. This is the only thing that got me home after I was so sick." She handed me a picture of a large cat. "Bless his heart," she mused. "The second time I went into the hospital, he ran off and grieved himself to death. He thought I was gone." Needless to say, the next picture was of a new cat called Spider.

As she shuffled through each one, it was like a childhood of flash cards: Melissa in a wheelchair . . . Melissa at Christmas time . . . Melissa with hepatitis . . . Melissa with a birthday cake. The young woman held in her lap her childhood that charted a course of mouth sores from medication, the inability to walk, and internal bleeding with stop-offs at depression and chemo.

As if she sensed what I was thinking, she said quietly, "These pictures are just part of my life. I mean, they made me strong just as cancer molded my life and made me strong."

But what about cheerleading and slumber parties? She was almost defensive. "They seem ridiculous to me—so silly now."

Didn't your graduation mean something special to you?

"It was just graduation day," she shrugged.

Her mother sitting nearby interrupted. "It was more special to her parents than it was to Melissa. Every day was just a miracle to us, but Melissa never thought she wasn't going to be here."

I suggested to her that there seemed to be some kind of pattern of resiliency among children regarding cancer. They face up quickly to what they've got. They don't bargain with it, set up time schedules, or sit around trying to figure out where to place the blame. They seem to say, "Okay! That's it! Let's get on with it. I've got a life to live here." Why?

"That's just a kid for ya," Melissa giggled. "They always think they got too much to do to let something like that bother 'em. Too many plans. That's just the way you are when you're a kid. You live for what's happening right now.

"I got a good one for you," she said, changing gears. "There was this girl who had to go quite often for chemo and one time she was kind of fed up, so she had some apple juice in her drawer and the nurse came in and told her to give her a urine specimen. So, the nurse went out and when she came back, she had poured a little of that apple juice in that cup and the nurse started to take it out when the girl said, 'It looks so cloudy, I think I'll filter it back through.' And she drank it! The nurse like to have had a heart attack.

"You gotta keep your attitude," she continued. "That's the big thing. I know it's a horrible situation. Especially when I relapsed. But you've got to make the best of it. When I was there [in the hospital] and I started to feel better, my attitude helped me and it helped other kids who were feeling sick."

Melissa tends to underplay the struggle. During one treatment, she lost her ability to walk and went into a wheelchair. From another medication, she got something akin to fever blisters on the inside of her mouth and down her esophagus. There were days of depression and mood swings and baths at crazy times of the day. She lost her hair twice.

With cancer behind her, Melissa's life has been on fast-forward. After having missed the entire fifth grade of school, she returned to catch up and graduate. She also started a teen support group of patients at Vanderbilt and was instrumental in bringing about the publication of a booklet on teens coping with cancer called "I'm Still Me!"

Following high school, she married a schoolmate and was divorced nearly three years later. She works as a bank teller but plans to go to Cumberland College in Lebanon to major in elementary education, following in her father's footsteps.

It's not true about faces being road maps that reflect routes of life you have traveled. Seeing Melissa and her mother, Judy, sitting there with the sun on them, it was hard to imagine a Christmas holiday nearly a decade ago when Judy Denney was driving her daughter home from the hospital. Melissa lay on the back seat of the car and never looked up or spoke a word. When they arrived home, Melissa went to her bedroom and pulled the curtains to spend the next couple of weeks in darkness and silence.

A few days before Christmas, Judy stood in the kitchen and realized her daughter had given up. "I was losing her," she said simply. "Each day she was getting a little sicker. One day I stood over the sink and said, 'God, I can't take it any longer. I've just gotta give her to you.' A short while later, Melissa called from her bedroom, 'Momma, can we go to town and look at the Christmas lights?' That was the turning point. From that moment on, she got stronger every day."

You would think that anger is a given when you're diagnosed. It would seem normal to demand an answer to "Why?" During the interview, I gave Melissa every opportunity to rail at someone for her misfortune. To doubt God's wisdom. To demand "Why?" She didn't take them:

"Cancer didn't change my life. I mean, it was just part of my childhood and the only thing it did was to make me more mature.

"They made it as good a home at Vanderbilt for me as they could. I was never angry. Confused and mixed up, yes, but never angry."

She sincerely believed this. Cancer to Melissa wasn't a rip or tear in the fabric of her existence. It was just another wrinkle. There would be more wrinkles to deal with in her life—maybe not as devastating, but they'd be important at the time. And she would survive them. She seemed to fight the obvious temptation to look back and dwell on what she had missed. Instead, she chose to look forward.

As she carefully returned the pictures to their assigned pockets, she said, "Here's one of Darth Vader and me. You know, from *Star Wars*? The cast visited the hospital. I thought I was in heaven. They sat around and talked to me. Things like that just bring you right out of bed, I don't care how sick you are."

I asked her if she realized how sick she was.

"The hospital gave me a little book that showed all the little cells with little faces and such that showed me basically there was an invader of some kind . . . kind of like something out of *Star Wars*."

Star Wars. Isn't that like a kid, I thought, to come up with something so simplistic for a condition so complex. I smiled one of those superior smiles that parents smile when they have the answer to something and their kids don't. Everyone knows cancer starts with a cell . . . actually, it's a bad cell that . . . I suppose it could be wearing a Darth Vader hat. . . .

I made a note to myself. "Find out what cancer is."

4

"What Have I Got?"

Emily was four and in chemotherapy. One day at the mall, she struck up a conversation with a woman who confided she had a cold. The woman then said to Emily, "How are you?" Emily responded matter-of-factly, "Oh, not so good. I have a runny nose, an owie on my foot, and a tumor."

> Emily, age 4
> Cincinnati, Ohio

What have I got?"

You have cancer.

It's a disease as old as dirt. In fact, it's prehistoric. Dinosaurs had huge tumors.

What you've got, one out of every four people in this country has got or will get. In 1989, 6,600 children will be diagnosed with it.

It has been described to some children as "weeds in your garden."

A few parents have suggested the Pac-Man principle where a group of bad cells gobble up the good ones.

Grandma probably refers to it in whispers as the "Big C." (When an adult says "He's very, VERY sick," you know the second "VERY" means cancer.)

Sometimes kids come up with their own mental picture of what it is. One depicted cancer as a large wave and he was on a surfboard trying to outrun it. Another saw it as a little bug and chemo as a hungry bear with big teeth ready to have its way with it.

Then there's twelve-year-old LT of Park Ridge, Illinois, who didn't have a clue what cancer was and didn't even care. He just fed some of his chemotherapy drug, hydroxyurea, to his plants for a science project and got second place. He said he was going to try for first place next year.

Ironically, most of the children I talked with had difficulty explaining what was going on inside them. The only thing they knew for sure was that the day they were diagnosed, it was like the first day of the Guilt Olympics.

Each member of the family lined up to compete

with one another to claim responsibility for this dreadful disease.

One father said he dropped Agent Orange from his helicopter in Vietnam, and he was sure he was responsible for his daughter's cancer.

Another father said he had smoked a fair amount of pot in college and was sure it had something to do with his daughter's illness.

A mother said she smoked a single cigarette when she was pregnant. Pick me!

A young brother of a cancer patient said he had once silently wished his brother dead so he could have his bike. He was sure he was being punished.

A ten-year-old said she got cancer "when I was still in my Mom's stomak [sic] and she went across this river and across the river was a power plant that caused my cancer."

And a grandmother offered this entry: "Do you think it could be because he wouldn't eat carrots? I told you he needed more vegetables." (Why do I have a gut feeling that the cause of cancer will never be anything that makes you thin?)

As one doctor said emphatically, "The one thing that is important for families to know from day one is that even if we knew that this was gonna happen, there is absolutely nothing that we could tell you that you should have done differently that would have made any difference because we just don't know where it [cancer] comes from. They need to know that."

So, why don't they understand what they've got?

Many people are intimidated by doctors. They feel intimidated by them because they look busy and sound breathless all the time. People also feel stupid when they don't understand what a doctor's talking about the first time around, so they don't ask again. And let's be honest here, people. English is not a doctor's first language.

If you go to a doctor often enough, after awhile you sorta figure out that when he says "I suggest the removal of superfluous apparel from your body so that you can conceal yourself under the disposable raiment of the abbreviated garment suspended on the back of the door," he means "Take your clothes off and get into that paper gown—the one that looks like a cocktail napkin."

Given that, I talked with Dr. Martin J. Murphy, Jr., director of the Hipple Cancer Research Center in Kettering, Ohio. In an interview that appears later in this book, I asked if he were explaining cancer to a child, what would he say?

Remember, English comes hard. He speaks fluent Medicalese.

"Cancer is a disease of the cells. The body is made up of cells and a cell is something so small we have to use a powerful microscope in order to see it, but even then we can't see all the things that make up a cell.

"Each of these cells is like a little world in itself.

It has its own driving force, it has its own identity. Some cells make hair, some cells make skin. So there are different cells in the body and each of them has its own little program. By putting all these cells together, it's now a community that participates for the good of the whole community or you the person, you the child.

"Something may have gone amiss or astray—we don't always know the reason for it. We know there are certain things that can cause an insult to a cell. It's insulted in that it does not die, but it changes. It changes the cell into a one-way street. It's irrevocable. It's a one-way direction. And that's called 'differentiation.' It's a big word and just means that the cells became different, that's all.

"And now the cell divides in a very special and strange way and a very dangerous way because we've got to stop it from dividing because if it continues to divide it's going to impact. That means it's going to invade the surrounding cells. Now, it doesn't gobble . . . cancer cells don't go around eating each other. Please get rid of that. What happens is that they crowd out . . . they literally displace all the surrounding normal neighboring cells that are trying to do their jobs.

"And if it's in the bone marrow, which is where the blood cells are produced . . . then we're going to find out that Johnny or Judy is sick because they're gonna have infections, they're gonna have colds and all of those things that we get when our blood is thick as a result of the lack of normal cells.

"It's those malignant cells that just keep dividing and dividing. We've got to stop them from invading, first of all, and stop them from spreading. We put boundaries on them, get 'em corralled as it were, stop them so the disease does not spread, then we concentrate on removing them, in this case with chemotherapy; killing those that are there until the last one is dead and when that happens, you'll be cured and you'll never again be confronted with that disease of that particular type."

Can you catch cancer?

"You'll catch a broken leg sooner than you'll catch cancer.

"Cancer is not communicable. We're not gonna catch it. Cancer cells are not transmittable. That's a fact. But what we can catch is a love of life from each other and that is what we gotta do when the diagnosis is made in a friend. Call that person immediately and say 'I don't know what to say,' but call them. Do not say 'Well, I don't know what to say,' and therefore we closet . . . we cocoon because we are afraid of saying the wrong thing or not saying enough. What we end up is not doing anything.

"And if we can break down this myth—the myth, in fact, the error, of the alleged transmittability of the disease, break that down and then say, 'All right, it's not transmittable, what do I fear from it?

Nothing.' What I have therefore is an opportunity to share my strength, my hope, my affection for that person."

And if you're a child explaining cancer to an adult, Jeff, a thirteen-year-old from Sedalia, Missouri, has a shorter, more visual version.

"My theory on leukemia is as follows.

"Just think of it as a factory of lights. Red lights stand for red blood cells, white blood cells are represented with white lights, and yellow lights are representing platelet cells.

"The lights go down the assembly line. Every once in awhile a light blows out because of a short in the wiring all the lights are hooked up to. So, the repairman is called up. His name is Chemotherapy. He goes through the wiring and repairs the short.

"After repairing the short, he goes through and looks for blown-out bulbs and lights. After finding the blown-out lights he replaces them. He waits around and make [sic] sure no more lights blow out. Then after all the work, he calls it a cure or a job well done.

"P.S. I think my lights are all burning and I hope I don't have any more blow-outs."

Most young patients reduce it to simpler terms than that. They call what they've got simply a "war."

Susan, of Tuscaloosa, Alabama, had liver cancer. She was left with a number of large scars on her stomach and right side. One day at kindergarten, several of her friends saw the scars and asked where she got them. She said, "Oh, I was wounded in the war," and then added, "and what a war it was."

In their minds, it's a real war. It goes beyond the daily chant, "What am I doing here?" It brings with it the loneliness of being cut off from friends, the risks and danger that each day brings for their survival, and the inevitable prayer, "When can I go home and pick up my life as it was?"

It doesn't really matter to them what the enemy looks like. They only know it has chosen them to attack.

As in a real conflict, there is a chain of command. There are the noncommissioned foot soldiers: Mom, who is in charge of KP and transportation; Dad, in charge of procurement and budget; brothers, sisters, and grandparents, who provide entertainment, do errands, and sit beside them in the trenches.

There are the "professionals" who make up the officers' staff. This includes nurses, therapists, social workers, support groups, camp directors, and heads of foundations that make wishes come true.

The generals are the doctors. They call all the shots in the campaign. They give orders that are to be obeyed without question. They assign duty that is tough at best. They send their troops into combat knowing there will be wounds, pain, and casualties. They grant them "leave" from the hospital one minute and take it back the next.

The general is the target for whatever good or bad that happens in this war. He didn't start it, he may hate it as much as his army, but he has the responsibility for getting his troops home—alive.

A teenager with cancer said that a friend of his who had been a Marine during three wars was asked how he could face fear for his own life for so many years and he replied, "I got to know the enemy well."

That's a problem in the cancer war. No one really knows it well—not even the generals. They just hit it with every weapon they've got and try to better the odds with each skirmish.

For whatever doctors are or are not, in the heat of the battle, they become the most important person in the life of a cancer patient.

I made plans to talk with one of the generals, Dr. Michael Amylon, who was on a two-week "maneuver" at Camp Okizu near Sacramento, California.

5

The General

*Her green eyes were intense as she took a
Rubik's cube out of her purse. "After the doctor
looks me over, I'm going to give him this cube.
If he can work it, then he can work on me."*

Lisa, age 12
Alpena, Michigan

The two-hour drive from the Sacramento airport to Camp Okizu gave me time to think.

I thought about Crystal of Grass Valley, California, who at age three had the perception to ob-
serve hospital procedure and said, "These people
don't know what they're doing. They put blood in
me one day and take it out another."

I thought about Becky, Tigard, Oregon, whose account of her doctor bristled with defiance. "He said I would never be able to walk again because I had such a small stump, but I did. I proved him wrong! I did walk again! He was really happy I had the nerve to do something brave and hard like that."

There was the pint-sized patient who sat on the examination table popping jelly beans and gazing forlornly at a dead plant on the doctor's windowsill. Her observation: "I hope he's better at taking care of people than he is his plants."

I thought about the letters that described their doctors as cold and inaccessible, and the crayon drawings where the kids fantasized about sticking a needle the size of a Masai spear into their doctors' backsides as revenge. I remembered the boy who advised, "If you happen to get a doctor who is snotty or doesn't want to answer your questions, change doctors!"

But there were other letters. Letters of unabashed love. Like Jason, Phoenix, Arizona, who wrote, "My doctor is a real cool dude. He calls me 'Squirrel Brains' but I knows he feels real bad sometimes."

Or the picture of a flowery heart drawn by Jessica, age six, who wrote, "Dr. Reynolds love me and I love him."

Maybe this kind of ambivalence goes with the command. Maybe doctors have to protect themselves behind a wall of aloofness and dispassion in order to survive.

I turned at the footbridge, and after a five-minute drive through tall pines and rows of cabins at Camp Okizu, I climbed to the top of the hill where Dr. Michael Amylon was quartered. It was a small room with a table, a couple of folding chairs, and a screen door that traffic never allowed to close.

He didn't look much like a general or, for that matter, like a repairman for cancer lights that short-circuited. Tall, lean, thirtyish, and dressed in faded jeans, he looked more like an ad for a soft drink.

This pediatric oncologist, who practices out of Stanford University Children's Hospital at Palo Alto, California, was readying for a mission. In a few minutes, he would hike down to the river and fish and canoe with a group of campers. Outside of a few cuts and mosquito bites, few of the campers would require his services as a doctor.

These kids weren't cancer patients. They just lived with a brother or sister who was. It was the first day of camp for "cancer siblings." They had already unpacked the usual array of shorts, T-shirts, underwear, rain gear, plus an unlimited supply of guilt, jealousy, and confused feelings.

I wondered what kind of emotional baggage Dr. Mike carried with him.

A native of New England, he went into oncology at Stanford because he liked the idea of a close relationship with a patient and the family over a long period of time.

He paid a big price for this relationship:

"A common defense mechanism," he explained, "is to create a kind of emotional distance. Some doctors don't allow themselves to feel. It's too hard. There needs to be enough doctors and enough nurses to take care of the kids and if some of them need to build a wall around themselves in order to continue doing that, then maybe it's okay. But I don't think that's really fair. I don't know how long I'll be able to continue, but I think that the family— the child especially—needs to be able to see you as a person during the hard times because the support that they need is more than just technical. I try real hard to be an accessible person.

"The kids have to know that I care about them and that I give them permission to be kids and I give their parents permission to let them be kids. I want them to be in school as much of the time as possible. I want them to be able to come to camp and show themselves they can still laugh and play and have fun.

"Kids are not supposed to be sick and they're not supposed to die. So I'm gonna do everything that I can to allow them to be children while they're going through this. Most of the kids are gonna get cured and you have to hang on to that or you couldn't survive in this field."

Do you cry a lot?

"A lot," he said flatly.

Dr. Mike had defied the first rule of a military engagement, the rule that says "Build a defense to protect your position. Have something between you and the enemy." Without a wall, he is vulnerable.

"I didn't fully appreciate how attached you really do get to the kids and how hard it is when . . . I thought I would be able to . . . but I still believe that it's important to let them have access to me as a person as well as a doctor. But I didn't think it would hurt so much."

Here was a doctor who treated children forty-eight weeks of the year. Another two weeks he volunteered at Camp Okizu for cancer patients. The remaining two weeks of the year he volunteered at Camp Okizu for the siblings.

I felt guilty somehow, asking him to defend the criticism that doctors seem "too busy" to talk:

"Parents will have questions and things that are bothering them that they don't ask because they perceive that we're too busy," he said, "and they don't think it's important. Well, we ARE that busy and there's always a lot going on. My attitude relaxes a lot when they go into remission and things are going well. But the parents are still very worried and I have to always try to keep that in mind.

"The parents are very protective of me as well as I try to be of them sometimes and they feel guilty asking questions and taking up too much time. I tell them at the beginning if there are things that are bothering them I want them to ask . . . to just say, 'Wait! Stop! I have a question!' "

What about counseling for their emotional ups and downs?

"Doctors can't do all that by themselves," he continued. "They don't have time. I think we have a responsibility to be aware of it and to lead them to another resource. Community support groups . . . family camp . . . they can't talk to their bridge partners about those things. They just wouldn't understand. The stresses on a family are terrible. And some families feel like somehow they're losing the battle if they admit that they need help."

Medals somehow would seem out of place on Dr. Mike's T-shirt. He probably wouldn't wear them anyway. But if he did, there would be one for the child he treated for seven years who later came into his office for a visit, bringing his wife and baby. There would be one for the kid, an amputee, he used to go skiing with—Dr. Mike just went to his wedding. And he would bask in the memory of the curly blond-headed little boy who came in every two weeks for his bone marrow, and after all the hurt inflicted on him, would grab Dr. Mike around the neck, hug him, and say "Thank you." ("I'd almost rather he got up and punched me in the nose!" said the doctor.)

As he talks, you can sense the awe and the pride

he has for his army of fighters . . . those little people who come into his office and ask to speak with him alone because they don't want to ask questions in front of their parents if it's going to make their mothers cry. He has no less compassion for the siblings, who were invited to a war they don't know how to fight.

"The sibs feel they're responsible for a lot of what's going on because they remember a time when they were bad and they should have been good and they're being punished.

"They worry that they themselves might get cancer because they don't know where it came from. They get shunted to Aunt Harriet's when the rest of the family's going to the hospital. They're not told about things because the parents perceive they can't really understand what's going on, so the sibs create all these fantasy images of what's happening—usually a lot worse than the reality. Kids can understand things an awful lot better than people give them credit for.

"Some of the younger kids will even develop physical symptoms that are very similar to what their brother or sister had before they were diagnosed because they see them getting all the attention and the presents and letters. Their grades go down. They really don't have many places where they can let all of that out and this is one of the places where they can.

"You know," he said smiling, "one of the

jealousies they have is about the friends that their ill sibling has at the hospital—a favorite nurse, a favorite doctor, all these people that they talk about all the time. And for the sibling to be able to go home and say they know Dr. Mike too is really important. I can carry them up the hill on my back and give them a story to tell."

As he prepared to leave, he added how the battleground of cancer was mined with surprises, some good, some bad. He smiled when he talked about their dark humor that never failed to astound him and that few adults understand. I told him about seven-year-old Douglas who said he wanted to write a book on cancer entitled, "Tha . . . Tha . . . That's 'All' Folks." He got the idea from the Looney Tunes cartoon.

Dr. Amylon shook his head. "I'm probably not the fastest wit on the block, but I do a lot of joking with the kids and they respond well to it. It makes them feel safer. If you can't laugh at yourself, who can you laugh at?

"They make terrible jokes," he continued. "Amputees carry their legs over their shoulders. They're riding down the freeway and they see somebody in another car looking at them and they lift up their wig. I think it's healthy."

6

The Chemo Cut

*When three-year-old Carrie's blond curls were
all gone and little fuzz was starting to grow
back, she observed with curiosity her father's
balding head as he bent over to tie her shoe.
"Daddy," she asked, "is your hair coming or
going?"*

Carrie's mother
Williamstown, Maine

When adults say things like "Having a sense
of humor about baldness is 'healthy,' " kids on chemotherapy must look at their hair sailing down the
drain and wonder how anyone can be this healthy
and still miss school.

Let's be honest here. The Chemo Cut is the pits!

It gives new meaning to the term "premature baldness." We're not talking E.T. here, who had a planet to go home to where everyone is hairless and has sixteen-inch fingers. We're talking about THIS planet where kids dedicate their lives to their hair.

I once figured out the hair of a teenager cost parents a nondeductible three thousand dollars a year. By the time you factor in the cost of shampoo, conditioner, bleach, creme rinse, mousse, gel, permanents, haircuts, styling wands, hair spray, curlers, color, ribbons, ornaments, and their own personal water heater, we could have bought our own nuclear power plant to pay for the electricity to run the hair dryer. Hair is that important. To use the worst pun in the free world, it is the "mane of their existence."

You're going to read a lot about courage in this book, but I am serious when I tell you that no courage is greater than that described on the pages of this chapter.

To many children of cancer, the loss of hair through chemo treatment is the final blow of indignity, the last layer of veneer that is stripped away leaving them naked and vulnerable to society. They have lost their place in a world where peer pressure lets you in . . . or keeps you out.

Tommy, a four-year-old from Buffalo, New

York, experienced a phenomenon we'll call "reverse peer pressure."

Tommy's mother spent days preparing her son for his inevitable loss of hair. Every time he'd yell "I need my hair!" she'd yell back "What for?" Finally, she convinced him he could go on breathing without it. He resigned himself to it and sat back to wait for the big chunks of hair that cling to the pillow at night or hug the drain on the shower floor. The day never came.

Tommy lost hair on his legs and arms, but the hair on his head remained intact. When he went to the clinic, he was "different." Everyone there was bald. They looked at him and wondered why he had hair. They talked about him. Some were even rude enough to ask him why he had hair. He wasn't one of them. He didn't look like them, relate to them, or feel that he belonged. About a year and a half into his treatments and after months of begging, his mother finally gave in and shaved his head.

Okay, so maybe his desire to be bald hinged on the fact that at age four, he hadn't had time enough to get seriously attached to his hair, but he got the peer pressure part right.

For awhile, Tommy loved being called "Baldy." But eventually, he came face to face with discrimination again. This time by those who had hair. Whenever he left his own "group," people would stare and make comments.

Everyone handles the Chemo Cut in his or her own way. Some wear scarfs, some take cover under hats, and some wear wigs. But the wigs are hot and the selection is limited, especially for children. Get real! Who wants to look like Eva Gabor when you're six years old? So the kids get pretty "creative" with their answers when someone asks "What happened to your hair?" These are some of them:

"I got sick of getting shampoo in my eyes."

"The wind just blew it out."

"My father is Kojak."

And I loved this one: "I just joined the Marines."

I couldn't resist adding some of my own. "What happened to your hair?"

"I sold it."

"Bad genes. My mother is bald."

"You'll never guess why I just fired my hairdresser."

"I traded it for this body."

"I was having a makeover and ran out of money."

When the Grateful Dead rock group brought its concert to Cape Charles, Virginia, Lynn saw possibilities for her bald head. Using magic markers, her friends drew the Grateful Dead logo on her skull and caused a mild sensation. Everyone at the concert thought it was far out and wanted to know how she ever got her mother to let her shave her head.

Lisa also had a flair for the dramatic. She was in a wheelchair in the hospital wearing a wig when two small patients stared at her. She stared back. Then she said, "Hey, you want to see what happens when you don't eat your vegetables?" With that, she whisked off her wig as the two kids darted back into their rooms. Later, Lisa told her brother, "I wonder what the dietitian will think when they have a run on broccoli?"

Another child became a walking billboard for Harley-Davidson when he transferred a decal onto the back of his head. David was entering his sophomore year at school and figured he'd let his T-shirt do the talking. The front of it read, "So what are you staring at . . . some of my teachers are bald too." When he turned around, the second part of the message read, "Only I'm better looking." It got him through some tough times.

If you don't believe that hair is for the birds, listen to Erin's story. After six months of chemotherapy to fight a kidney tumor, the four-year-old lost her hair. A hairdresser and friend of the family suggested she save it and put it out for the birds so they could use it to make nests. Once the word got out, Erin became a clearinghouse for everyone who cut their hair.

Five months after she started collecting everyone's hair, a park ranger took her out to the state park to see if her loss had been the birds' gain. Sure enough, they found several nests with Erin's recycled hair.

Being bald in a hairy world isn't easy—even for adults. Sportscaster and author Joe Garagiola told Johnny Carson one night he hated it when people asked him when he lost his hair. "They act like I've misplaced it," he said. "Or worse, they wonder why I don't go for a cure for baldness. It's not a disease like athlete's foot or a headache. And how many times can you laugh at 'Hey Joe, you know what stops falling hair? The floor!'?"

Carl Reiner, a hairless actor-producer, has made up his own rules about baldness. "Anyone who wears hair during the daytime is overdressed," he said.

Many find that humor somehow surfaces in the darkest hour. Take Samantha. She was a certified thumbsucker and hair twister who, after five months of chemo, lost most of her hair and "twisting" became a major challenge.

One evening as she readied for bed, she begged her mother to sleep with her. Her mother used her seventeen reasons not to, ending with the one that has always worked with kids: "Gee, Mommy and Daddy have to share a bed, but you're so lucky you get a bed all to yourself." Samantha wasn't buying. She still wanted to sleep with her mother. Finally, her mother turned to her daughter, exasperated, and said, "Samantha, give me one good reason why I should sleep with you."

With large brown eyes she looked up and said, "Because I don't have enough hair to twist and you do!"

The good news is that hair is a perennial. It comes up year after year. So you have a bad season and lose a crop of hair to chemo. One day you'll see a shoot surface, followed by a field of fuzz, until one day your mother will be banging on the bathroom door, reminding you that your three-thousand-dollar head of hair is overbudget and if you don't stop washing it so often, you'll be bald.

Mothers. Where do they come up with this stuff?

7

What's a Mother For?

*At one of David's checkups I took one look at
his lung x-ray and everybody in the room
noticed the color leave my body. There was an
obvious large shadow. His oncologist took one
look at me and said, "It's okay, Mrs. Peterson,
that's David's heart you're looking at."*

David's mother
Two Rivers, Wisconsin

WANTED: Woman to raise, educate, and
entertain child for minimum of twenty years. Be
prepared to eat egg if the yolk breaks, receive anything in hand child spits out, and take knots out of
wet shoestrings with teeth. Must be expert in making costume for "bad tooth" and picking bathroom

locks with shish kebab skewer. Seven days a week, twenty-four hours a day, including holidays. Comprehensive dental plan, vacation, medical benefits, and company car negotiable.

If there were a job description for motherhood, that would be close. If the job description included mothers of kids with cancer, you would have to add: An additional forty hours a week set aside for reading magazines in doctor's waiting room, chauffeuring child to and from treatments and therapy, standing in line getting prescriptions filled, and running errands. Sustaining guilt for not giving enough to other members of the family. Major worrying twenty-four hours a day. Must possess maturity to realize that you can't "kiss cancer and make it well."

All of it sounds like the old ad they used to run for Pony Express riders: "DUTY IS HAZARDOUS. ORPHANS PREFERRED." But mothering is survivable. It just takes conditioning and an emotional yo yo with a long, strong string.

Worrying is a priority. Estelle, a mother from Path, Rhode Island, succeeded in elevating it to an art form. "As a parent, it was my duty to worry. As the parent of an oncology patient, I perfected it. I would keep lists in case I forgot one. With each new piece of information, I would revise the list, developing intricate new worries.

"Within a six-year period I had a list of 142 things to worry about. Six actually happened, including two that were not even on my list. I guess

I wasn't as efficient as I thought I was, but I keep practicing."

Practice! Practice! Practice! Tommy's mother of Buffalo, New York, was hysterical when Tommy fell flat on his face while crossing the street. "Tommy! Tommy! What's wrong? Why can't you walk?" He looked up and said, "Because my shoe-string is untied."

When Steve started to scream from his room in the hospital, his mother in the hallway alerted the emergency room staff, who raced to his bedside with their equipment only to find Steve watching a ballgame and explaining, "It was a bad call on Yaz" (Carl Yastrzemski of the Boston Red Sox).

Raising children who do not have a life-threatening disease has some shaky rules at best, but at least there are rules. With a sick child, there are few guidelines and you don't know which rules to keep and which ones to toss out.

When your twelve-year-old daughter with leukemia confronts you on her way to a dance in the school gym with, "Momma, do you honestly think anyone will dance with a twelve-year-old bald-headed girl?" how do you answer her?

You're doing the best you can when one day your child's doctor challenges you with "You think Sam is going to die, don't you?" When you shout No!, he says, "Then why are you treating him as if he were?"

How do you deal with the ambivalence when

you yell at your son in the morning for bleeding on the carpet, yet sit in his room at night as he sleeps just watching and wanting to be near?

How do you handle the anger of hearing just one more smiling-faced, thoroughly well-meaning person say, "I don't know how you've done it. You've been through so much"—like you had a choice.

There's the usual advice from mothers who have been there and know what they're talking about: "Get your rest, let your husband handle some of the burdens of the treatment, try to talk to someone about something else besides cancer and buy yourself something whether you need it or not . . . indulge yourself and don't lose your sense of self."

But mostly, it's telling yourself there is nothing you can do to change your situation, so you hang on to all the normalcy and humor you can get.

In the chain of command in this war, mothers are responsible primarily for transporting and feeding the troops who fight the disease each day. Sounds simple, doesn't it? Everyone knows children are picky eaters. Normally, they won't eat anything mothers pack in a paper sack with their name on it or any food that hasn't danced on TV.

But the eating habits of kids with cancer run the gamut from eating one banana a day and throwing that up while he or she is in chemo to going through a condition we call the "prednisone pigout."

Prednisone is a drug that reacts differently on different people, but on some, the side effect is an insatiable appetite . . . like an Orson Welles wish. Providing food to a child on this drug could become an aerobic exercise for mothers.

Some kids have the pizza parlor's phone number memorized. It is not unusual to scarf down three hamburgers, a chocolate shake, and french fries at one sitting only to finish it off with a couple of turkey sandwiches, a half a pie, and a dish of pasta.

Some awake lusting for garlic chip dip and potato chips at 1:00 A.M. Others request broccoli for breakfast without blinking an eye.

If we were giving medals for patience and stamina, Jeanne, a mother from Woburn, Massachusetts, would be right there in the top ten.

Her son, Bobby, was diagnosed as having leukemia at age three and when he became thin and weak, his doctor prescribed prednisone because he thought it would improve his appetite. He warned it would probably cause mood swings.

"Well," thought Jeanne, "I'd gladly put up with mood swings if it would improve his appetite."

They had no sooner hit home when Bobby announced, "I'm hungry. Get me oatmeal—instant oatmeal and cinnamon toast." Jeanne gladly prepared it. "He ate quickly and with a serious expression on his face, similar to that of a wild animal feeding on prey," she observed. "When he finished he said, 'More toast.'"

Nine slices later, Jeanne was out of bread and was ordered to go to the store. She talked him into eggs and as she was preparing them he snatched a bowl of gelatin out of the refrigerator. As she put the last spoon into the dishwasher, he boosted himself up to the freezer and came out with three frozen pops. After inhaling them, he rested.

"My once-pleasant little boy had his mood swings to that of a hungry animal," she said. "He continually stalked the kitchen. One day when he was particularly weak, he got to the refrigerator by wagon, pulled by his two-year-old brother." (She enclosed a picture of an adorable toddler pushing an equally adorable child in a little red wagon.)

"He hid hot dogs in his overalls pockets, he sneaked cheese into the living room while I was in the bathroom. Neighbors and relatives were 'robbed' of their cold cuts when we visited.

"When the doses were lowered and his therapy became regulated, he had treatment for three weeks and the fourth week was a rest. During that fourth week of the cycle, Bobby would develop a main craving of one particular food. One week it was whipped cream. Then suddenly he'd switch from whipped cream to corn on the cob. Which wasn't exactly plentiful in January in Massachusetts," said Jeanne.

"He often awoke in the middle of the night to eat. He had a week of craving pork fried rice, which kept my husband running back and forth to the

Chinese restaurant. One morning at 3:00 A.M. I found myself leaning on my kitchen table, supporting my head with my arm, while my somber-faced son sat opposite me waiting impatiently for the toaster oven to finish warming the rice."

There is not a woman who has suffered from morning sickness who will not empathize with Jeanne. She was two months pregnant when Bobby developed a love affair with chicken drumsticks or "meat on the bone" as he referred to it. He had it at every meal, and at breakfast one morning in the hospital, Bobby sat eating "meat on the bone" while Jeanne hung her head out of the eighth-story room sucking in "chicken-free air" and moaning, "Oh Lord, have mercy on me."

The second year was easier as Bobby went into his fruit and vegetable cycle. Along with his diet, his moods began to improve.

In February of his second year in therapy, it snowed heavily in Massachusetts. Jeanne bundled up the boys and began rolling snowmen on the front lawn. They put a head on "Frosty" and she went inside to get some chocolate cookies for eyes. Bobby had his own ideas. When Jeanne returned outside, she noticed Frosty with a carrot nose and two carrots stuck in his backside. Bobby held her hand and said proudly, "Frosty's getting a bone marrow and a spinal tap." It was a snowman he could relate to.

Bobby had come a long way. A year ago, his snowman would have been standing there in the buff—Bobby would have eaten the carrot nose and the needles for his spinal tap and bone marrow.

"There certainly isn't anything funny about cancer," said Jeanne, "but it did bring about situations that were quite humorous . . . especially looking back at it now."

I've saved worshipping at the Shrine of Perpetual Guilt until last because mothers (who invented guilt) have devised more ways to punish themselves than any other species on the earth. They visit the shrine daily laying at its feet such wondrous questions as, "How could I have permitted this to happen to my child?" "What kind of a mother am I who can laugh at a Bette Midler film when her child has cancer?" "I have no right to question God about how long I have to endure living like this." "Forgive me. I locked the bathroom door again and pretended I wasn't there." The list goes on.

Mothers are programmed to bring a child to maturity and by all that is holy they will use everything they have to bring this about. Their determination . . . their fight . . . their courage . . . their love . . . are invested without question. There is no force on earth quite as powerful as a mother struggling to restore her child to its original perfection—no matter what it takes.

She is not unlike the story of the Jewish grandmother who took her grandson to the beach one day, complete with bucket, shovel, and sun hat. The grandmother dozed off and as she slept, a large wave dragged the child out to sea. The grandmother awoke and was devastated. She fell to the ground on her knees and prayed, "God, if you save my grandchild I promise I'll make it up to you. I'll join whatever club you want me to. I'll volunteer at the hospital, give to the poor, and do anything that makes you happy."

Suddenly, a huge wave tossed her grandson on the beach at her feet. She noticed color in his cheeks and his eyes were bright. He was alive. As she stood up, however, she seemed to be upset. She put her hands on her hips, looked skyward, and said sharply, "He had a hat, you know."

Mothers of these sick children don't want to hear this, but generally they are an impressive force who possess all the human frailties and flaws we all possess, but somehow they rise above them . . . laughing when they can and crying when they must.

There is no major, one-way, well-paved super six-lane highway to survival, dotted with rest stops, facilities, free road maps, and other travelers to offer advice on conditions ahead. Everyone must travel her own route to get where she wants to be.

When Sandra Bakun arrived at her destination, she found she was not the same woman she was when she started the trip.

But then, most mothers aren't.

A Mother's Vigil

They were driving home from Boston when Jill declared in no uncertain terms she wasn't going through it all again. Her cancer had returned and she wanted no part of it. She was not going to take her medication. She was not going for her treatments. She was not going to lose her hair again.

"Then you're committing suicide!" yelled her mother. "I don't want you to die. I'll tie you to a chair and stuff it [medicine] down your throat! You're talking about losing your stupid hair! We're talking about your life!"

Somehow, it was hard to imagine that this tall (5'11"), slim, soft-spoken woman sitting across from me in a Boston hotel room had ever raised her voice. Even the speech didn't seem to fit.

But it wasn't an ordinary day for Sandra Bakun or her daughter. After battling leukemia for six years, Jill relapsed and that day Sandra became a force that even she didn't recognize. Maybe for the first time she realized cancer wasn't going to be an interim—it was going to be as much a part of her life as breathing. She could drown in it or she could learn to swim.

At forty-six, Sandra Bakun has spent nearly two-thirds of her married life administering to a child with cancer. For seventeen years, her emotions have soared and plummeted like a roller coaster through two diagnoses, two remissions, and a relapse.

The struggle of Jill, her two sisters, her brother, and her father are all stories of special courage. This, however, is the story of a mother who was invited to stand "watch" in a war and knows she can never go home again.

Like any veteran, Sandra can resurrect her life in "peacetime" on cue. It's like an old, familiar picture that you carry in your billfold to remind you what you're fighting for.

Married at nineteen, she was a traditional housewife and mother of four children living in Stow, Massachusetts, a suburb thirty miles outside Boston. She worked for the League of Women Voters, sat on the washer to keep it in balance when there were gym shoes in the spin cycle, and dealt with the trauma of the week: "Peter fell down the cellar stairs and had to have stitches in his chin and I thought I was not a good mother for allowing that to happen." Traditional.

On the side, to keep her sanity, Sandra wrote a column for a local newspaper from her home. "One day we had a terrible blizzard and I did this stupid column about how mothers survived the blizzard with the kids home. But mostly it was a society column. I wasn't making much money, but it was fun. I was just a country mouse," she shrugged.

The first volley in the war was fired in 1971.

Her husband, Jimmy, held his frightened six-year-old daughter, Jill, in his arms as the doctor inserted the long needle into her lower hip, removing a portion of the precious bone marrow.

Jill was diagnosed as having acute lymphocytic leukemia. They trudged home with their secret, wondering what lay in their future. But Stow is a small town and its people responded with a bank book containing two thousand dollars and a brochure about Disney World. They wanted the Bakuns to have one last hurrah.

Surrounded by twirling tea cups and dancing bears at Disney World, the Bakuns tried to prepare themselves for what lay ahead. As Sandra wrote, "The children were entranced by the enchanted world and the constant excitement. It was the right thing to do. Not to forget our situation, but to appreciate our brief interludes with life. It was there that my husband and I decided that life was worth a risk, and it was there that our roots for strength for whatever would lie ahead were put down."

But Disney World is a fantasy. When the lights go out and the rides shut down and the costumes no longer have bodies in them to bring them to life, the magic is gone. For the Bakuns, Adventureland became a quest for "normalcy"; Frontierland turned into a new treatment for Jill; Fantasyland was a day without thinking about cancer; and Tomorrowland was iffy at best.

The marriage that had worked so well BE-

CAUSE Jimmy was light and funny and had always complemented Sandra's serious side now sent them into opposing camps. "I figured you just save yourself and go your opposite ways," remembers Sandra.

By her own admission, Sandra "ate, drank, and thought cancer, cancer, cancer" every day of her life. She figured if she armed herself with all the knowledge she could gather she could handle anything. Doctors say this is not uncommon for mothers to share the disease by making it a part of them.

She became active in Candlelighters, a support group of other families facing cancer. She investigated a dump site three blocks from her house that purportedly was under scrutiny for contaminant violations. (None were found.) She had her own well water tested. She frequented the library to find out all she could about the disease and wrote down her questions for later discussions with the doctor.

When her daughter lost her hair and wore a wig, Sandra wore one too. She kept a day-by-day diary of the disease. At one point, she became a school nurse for two days a week because she wanted to be near Jill. She directed a lot of her anger at her husband because she felt he wasn't with her. She felt alone. "Jimmy said his faith was so strong he knew Jill would make it, but it only made me feel that my faith wasn't strong enough and I had to depend on science."

Jimmy handled the problem in his own way.

He didn't mind that Sandra attended a lot of meetings. "He never complained if his supper wasn't ready on time," she said. "He would go off in his direction to his hobbies. He thought this [cancer] was mine. It became my obsession."

A few months after Jill's diagnosis, Jimmy was hospitalized with chest pains that were attributed to stress. The visits to the doctors when he would hold Jill down through her bone marrow treatment plus the loss of his job due to technology took their toll. But in 1977, a new blow struck the already walking-wounded family.

After six years of remission, cancer reappeared. Jill was in relapse and began her treatments from square one.

So did her family.

On the way home from Boston on that day, Sandra went from a woman who "felt like a complete jerk" because she was afraid to ask the doctor a question to a woman who was to testify before the Massachusetts legislature against the legalization of laetrile.

Sandra emerged from a shy woman who had never even driven a car into Boston to a woman who lied to get a job running a dictaphone and when they asked her to take a test, said without blinking, "I've forgotten how to turn it on."

"I was always a serious person," admitted Sandra, "and I keep saying I became unbalanced because it was true. I passed over the center and was consumed with my daughter's illness.

"My older daughter, Jean, has told me that she felt neglected and I really feel bad about that. Sometimes Julie would come up and say, 'I scraped my knee,' and I guess I wasn't very compassionate to her. I passed it off as a piddly little thing. I didn't realize what I was doing because when you're faced with leukemia everything else is just minor. Mononucleosis is minor. But I think I've told Jean, my older daughter, that if it happened all over again, I don't think I would have done anything any differently, that I did my best and I thought I was a good mother, and I'm sorry if I didn't do it all right. She has to forgive me for that. She has to because I did the best I could.

"Today, I'm much more mellow and mature," she smiled. "I appreciate life so much, every little thing. I'm in the Deadline Decade," she laughed.

"You know, in Gail Sheehy's book *Passages*? I skipped over the twenties and thirties. At forty-six, I'm in the period of life where you don't worry anymore about what people think. I'm me! This is the time if you don't do it now, you're never gonna do it. So I go out and if I like a dress, I buy it. I always felt guilty, like 'Wait, I shouldn't do that. Look at the price.' Always a bargain hunter. I still do bargains but I'll buy it only if I like it. I've changed. My life is not totally kids. When my son comes home from college with all his dirty clothes, I say, 'Now you wash 'em. I'll show you how to run the washer.' "

For the first time in years, Sandra is allowing herself the luxury of a future. She fantasizes about writing the great American novel when she "retires to Cape Cod." She has plans to turn her attention to the survivors of cancer who suffer from job discrimination and insurance inequities.

Sandra once wrote, "When the quantity of life looks safe—quality takes precedence." She is testing that theory.

At present, all the Bakuns are in remission, so to speak, and have gotten on with their lives. Jill is a child life specialist working with children with cancer. She is twenty-three years old.

It's a great temptation to read about the Bakun family and imagine how you would handle it. How you would gather around the kitchen table like Donna Reed and her husband Dr. Stone and conduct a family council to "bond and share feelings." (Maybe Madonna would make a guest appearance as a social worker.) All the devastation that entered your lives would be arranged neatly according to priorities and would be resolved within twenty-four minutes, with six minutes of messages from your sponsors.

But this is not a television sitcom. This is real life. "It's that Damocles syndrome, the sword hanging over your head," observed Sandra, "but you go on."

It was late. Sandra had a long trip back to Stow to make that night. As if to leave on a high note, she paused at the door and flashed a warm smile. "You know, I don't even mind being tall anymore."

8

What Are Fathers For?

"June! I'm home!"

Ward Cleaver, father
"Leave It to Beaver" television series

Can you imagine being so invisible you have to announce your presence when you walk in the door? It has always been the perception of Dads from Jim Anderson of "Father Knows Best" to Jason Seaver on "Growing Pains" . . . from Ozzie's greeting to Harriet to Jack Arnold walking through "The Wonder Years."

They're fathers who rarely have starring roles in the chronicles of family life. They come home, turn off a few lights, read the paper, eat dinner, scratch the dog behind the ears, and go to bed. If a demolition ball like cancer hits the family while they're gone, it's business as usual.

"I'm a salesman and I'd be driving down the highway and I'd pull over and bawl for forty-five minutes or I'd be talking with a customer and all of a sudden I'd just walk out and get in the car and leave."

Fathers have a reputation for going through life like they have bodies shot full of novocaine. They're cool. They have a certain dignity and distance to maintain—no matter what.

"My Dad won a trip to Orlando, Florida, for me when he entered a Jell-O Gelatin Jump. For this he had to jump into four hundred gallons of Strawberry Jell-O. I never thought my Dad would do this."

Fathers are also endowed with a strength and detachment that permits them to witness harsh situations and not fall apart.

When Ken decided to share responsibilities with his wife he accompanied his daughter, Mary Beth, to her spinal tap. When Mary Beth groaned, Ken turned white as a sheet and fainted dead away.

So much for Father Teresa and so much for the three popular myths surrounding fathers. The truth is men are just as vulnerable, just as caring, just as devastated as their wives when cancer strikes their children.

But the male species is elusive. The outpouring of feelings I had hoped to assemble in a folder marked "DADS" never materialized. When I opened the white envelope it looked like the one our son had marked "INCOME TAX RECORDS"— there wasn't a scrap of paper in it.

In my inquiries, fathers began to take on a "rare bird" dimension. "Is it true you spotted a three-piece-suited Father last week? Does he talk?" "You had a male-breasted Father at camp and didn't call me?" "I know there are thousands of species of Dad Childwatchers out there, but where do they flock?"

In June 1988, three fathers were sighted in Portland, Oregon. All three had daughters with cancer and had become friends through Candle-lighters events. I flew to Portland where we dined over prime rib and a tape recorder. They had all lived with cancer long enough to be comfortable talking about it.

Their perspective was not the same as those of mothers.

Fathers have traditionally been the ones who parked the car in the rain, took the family picture, checked out noises in the basement, or put the dog to sleep. They are charged with keeping things moving. Their roles in cancer are much the same. They have to carry on business as usual—going to work each day and wondering what is happening in their absence.

Bill Warbington, sales representative for Industrial Rubber and Supply Company, whose daughter, Erin, lost her leg to Ewing's sarcoma in 1985 when she was eight years old, said, "Sometimes I thought it would be a lot easier if I could send Jan out and I could stay home. It's harder being gone. You feel such rage. Something is happening to your family and you can do nothing about it. If it's a guy across the street harassing your little girl, you can go rip his throat out, but this you can't do a thing about. Cry in front of your child? No. See, this is the thing. Growing up you can't give away your guts. When you're a little kid in junior high school, college, whatever, and you do something wrong and the coach stands there and screams in your face, what's gonna happen if you start crying because you're upset?

"Or if you're in the military and the sergeant started pounding on your butt or the lieutenant colonel comes down on you. Are you gonna start crying? You can't do that. I mean the male is taught that you get hurt physically and emotionally or someone takes something away from you, something you can't do anything about, but you don't stand there and cry. You just don't."

His friend, Ken Raddle, vice president of national sales for Young American in Portland, is the father of Mary Beth, who was diagnosed in 1984 at age eleven as having acute lymphocytic leukemia.

"Poor mothers get beaten to a pulp and it's just really difficult to be a mother. Much more difficult than being a father because I'm the guy who comes home after work and I listen to the version of Mary Beth not getting her stuff fast enough or getting her blanket when she is too hot/too cold, why aren't you doing it faster and then, 'Oh, here's Dad,' with a big smile."

The third member of the trio is Bob Kreinberg, customer service and district director for Nike. His daughter, Sarah, was diagnosed in 1979 at the age of fifteen months with a brain tumor. "When Penny [his wife] and I went into the Peace Corps, the minister who married us said, 'This experience has the reputation of making or breaking marriages. Because of it—and again it's one of those things where you're totally cut off—you're forced to deal with one another.' Cancer takes that situation and intensifies it about twenty times because you don't have a choice. We've learned a lot about ourselves."

Sitting there listening to their emotions that came spilling out like a dam of water that had been held back, they didn't seem like such enigmas. But I remembered a little girl who said she had a memory that would stay with her forever. "One time," she smiled, "when I was really sick, my Dad brought food to me and when I couldn't eat it, my Dad cried. I had never seen him cry before."

And there was the small boy who said he went sailing down the hallway in his wheelchair in the hospital with his father racing alongside him dragging the IV. He added, "We've never had so much fun."

There was the mother who said bitterly, "My husband denied it all. He just wanted it to go away. It's a male trait where they think everything is going to turn out right because they want it to turn out right. He said he didn't need a support group. How do you think that made me feel?"

And another one observed, "My husband was very inquisitive and intellectual and that was his way of, I'm sure, insulating himself from the pain. The 'I'm in charge. I'll ask the questions. I won't break down.' But I resented that quite a bit of the time."

Fathers may not record diaries of their child's illness. They may not even talk about it. Many won't begin to network with one another. But you have only to listen to them share their helplessness and their pain to know they aren't as isolated from the problem as people think they are.

"I've learned it's arrogant to think we're going to live forever," said Ken. "Everything is valuable. It's been a privilege to have Mary Beth in our family as it is with any of our children. They're not really ours and for us to think they're gonna be with us and live longer than us is arrogant.

"I've learned a lot from Mary Beth. That no matter what's happened in your day, you go ahead and give 'em a hug in bed at night. I was saying to Sharon [his wife], 'My God, Mary Beth's gonna get married someday and I'm gonna be on her honeymoon saying prayers with her.'"

It was late in the evening when we adjourned to Ken's living room to continue the conversation. The "M" word had not been spoken. It was time. "What about money?" I asked.

They looked at one another like "Who wants to tell her?" It was their job in this war and it was a killer. Finding the money to pay for a catastrophic disease was a burden all three of them wore like a bad suit. Bob took the plunge. "The trouble is families affected with cancer have twenty-five percent of their incomes or something like that going to support the illness. I have a pretty good insurance plan. It's covered a lot of things, but there's a lot of incidentals, a lot of things that aren't covered. There's also a lot of things you tend to do to compensate for the illness. You compensate by taking the kids special places. We went to Disneyland. That's kind of an expensive operation for a family of five to try to do, and had expenses of travel, expenses of having to deal with the other kids in situations where they're out of the home . . . a lot of that kind of thing.

In a lot of cases, where families are ripped apart, I think the pressure becomes one of those, 'What are you gonna do?' "

He paused and held out his hands helplessly as if there were a need to explain. "We were given five percent odds of our daughter making it through. We had no other choice."

"I said, 'To hell with it,' interrupted Bill. "We're gonna start doing what's important to all of us while we're all still here.

"Jan was averaging ten hours a week trying to keep the insurance company from screwing us out of the coverage. At least ten hours a week! They paid one hundred percent to amputate, then what came after there was not full coverage. They'll take off your leg, but then their attitude is, 'Leg's gone, don't worry about that. You'll still grow up."

"My attitude was, 'I'm never gonna make enough money to pay this thing off anyhow, so what they gonna do? They can't take the same thing away from me twice. We're gonna start doing what's important to all of us."

Ken was nodding vigorously. "We went through a personal bankruptcy just two years prior to Mary Beth's diagnosis. We had stress in our relationship almost greater than the cancer. Sharon had to balance almost a full-time job, leaving work at any moment, taking lots of days off, and then dealing with the financial stress as well. We used all the money we had set aside for our oldest daughter to go to college. We had used just everything we had."

Under normal circumstances, these three men would probably never have met. Their common ground was three little girls fighting for their lives and needing all the support they could get. They talked about another father who had been invited to attend a Candlelighters social event.

"The one who refused to get out of the car and wanted food sent to him?" asked Bill.

"That's the one," said Bob. "I think he thought we just sat around talking about cancer all night."

"I told 'em to take him the food," said Ken quietly. "He needs time. He'll join us . . . when he's ready."

On the flight home I thought not only about the mothers and the fathers I had talked with, but the reams of feelings chronicled on yellow tablets, written in longhand . . . the ink sometimes smeared with tears . . . little drawings, eulogies, pictures, holy cards, and emotions so real and so private it hurt to read them.

I remembered the mother who said, "Mark didn't receive the Heisman Trophy, but he received a courage trophy for his braveness. He didn't graduate magna cum laude from Harvard, yet he finished and passed first grade. He didn't become a nationally recognized Eagle Scout hero, yet in ten months he was in the Tiger Club and the blue ribbon he received for just participating in the Pinewood

Derby Car Race was an accomplishment. Cancer is sad, but it's not the end of the world. I feel I owe Mark."

Or the one who so eloquently summed up her life. "Most parents of children with cancer will speak to you of the specialness of that time of their lives. We were living on the edge, emesis basins, dangerously low white counts, Visa and Mastercharge, we all knew the battlefield, but we also knew the trenches—treats from the pharmacy, giggly nights telling riddles till we gagged ourselves, direct emotional experiences of deepest love and deepest rage, prayers to a God we barely knew but were counting on. So . . . life goes on. I believe these special children give us an incredible faith in God— if we let them."

In nearly every instance, there had been some positive changes in the lives of the people around these children.

What are children, really? Are they something "issued" to parents like an IRA that is invested in to reap dividends? Are they pieces of putty to be molded in your own image, and when you don't like what you create, you discard? Or are they insurance policies that you sign up for as protection for care in your old age? (My kids always believed I wanted personal live-in slaves.) They are none of these things. Children are "awarded" for an indefinite length of time over which you have no control. All children are born under these terms. There are no guarantees that you will have physically perfect children or that they will outlive you.

What they were saying was, these children had a specialness they wouldn't have missed for anything in the world. The real sadness would have been if these children had never been at all.

By Alfy Vince

By Heather Vaughn

Mark Can Do it !! :) without Crying

Monday	Tuesday	Wednesday	Thursday	Friday
Walk to Travis' house 3 times a day	Walk to Travis' house 3 times	Walk to Travis' house 3 times	Rode bicycle walked some at hospital and around inside and outside	
Get dressed with help	Get dressed with help	Get dressed	Got dressed by himself	
Sofa Exercises -Leg Raises -Tummy Bends	Sofa exercises -Leg Raises -Tummy Bends	Sofa exercises -Leg Raises -Tummy Bends	Sofa exercises -Leg Raises -Tummy bends	
Breathing Exercises	Breathing Exercises	Breathing Exercises	Breathing Exercises	

By Mark Fite

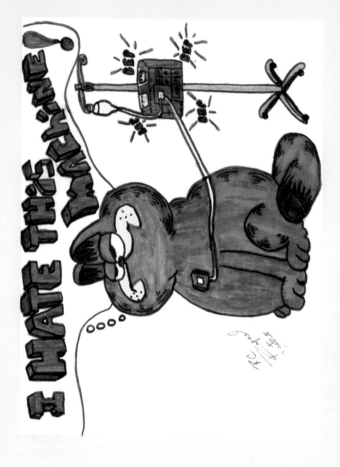

By Rafael Castro

By Sybil Cox

By Holly Vaughn

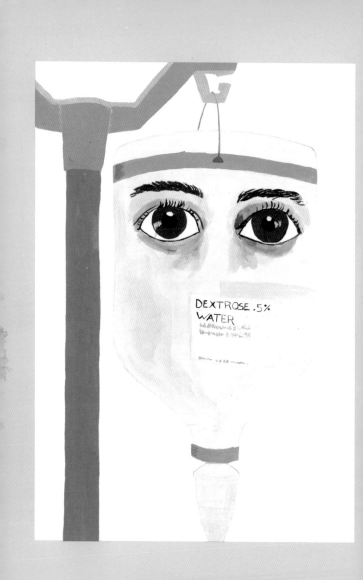

By Aaron Asencio

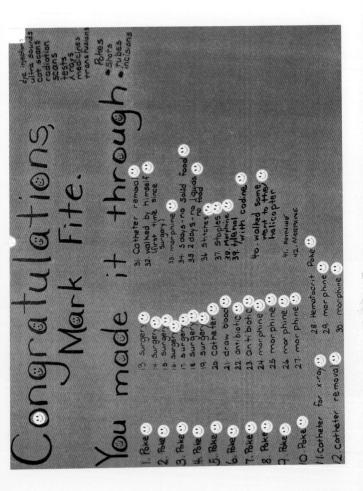

By Mark Fite

By Betsy Sweet

- We Sing "Looney Tunes" on the way to Camp -

By Lauren Cowell

High adventure

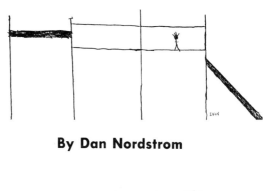

By Dan Nordstrom

By Joy Anderson

What has 6 legs, 4 eyes, 2 heads and a tail? A hors and his rider. HAHA

By Kelly Delk

By Kelly Delk

By Zach Davis

Camp Reach for the sky

by
Levi
Considine

By Levi Considine

By Ryan Bigger

A Hopelet, by Stephanie Summerix

HOPE

COURAGE

By Brett Howey

By Kristi Correa

9

What Are Friends For?

"Get well, David, we all like you but one person."

> Letter to David, a cancer
> patient from Portage, Michigan,
> from a classmate

Everyone knows what a "best friend" is.

A best friend never goes on a diet . . . when you're fat!

She pretends she doesn't know the answer when you haven't studied.

He'll give you the "first lick" off his ice cream cone.

When you go to a dance in the gym together and she gets a better offer, she'll leave with you.

When you're sick and miss the Michael Jackson concert, he won't have a good time.

For more than forty years, I have had such a friend.

When I gave myself a home permanent and left it on too long, she was the only one to sit with me in the bathroom until it grew out.

When I told my best friend my husband gave me two snow tires for our anniversary, she never said, "You should be happy he remembered."

When I was pregnant and my stomach looked like a snack tray on a car door at the drive-in, she never said, "There's a glow about pregnant women."

When I had a miscarriage and everyone else in the world said, "There will be other babies," she cried with me over the one I had lost.

When I moved three thousand miles away, she never once told me what I was doing to her. When her mother died, I never said, "She had a rich, full life and was in her seventies."

When her political candidate lost and mine won, I never said, "Ha, ha, I told you so."

Every time we got together, neither of us had to say, "I'm glad to see you."

A few years ago, my best friend lost her youngest child. He was in his twenties. I listened to her. I cried with her. I felt pain that I had never known I could feel before. But not once did I say to her "I know how you feel."

Having said all those wonderful things about myself, I will now tell you that when I first heard of his death I didn't want to call her or meet her face to face. In spite of our closeness of forty years, I didn't know what to say or how to act. I felt a strangeness—like I didn't know her anymore. My first words to her were "What can I do?" Her eyes brimmed with tears as she said simply, "Be my friend."

I nodded knowingly, but later I thought, "How do I do that?"

What do people who are ill and their families *want* from their friends? I've read hundreds of letters from families where cancer has entered their lives and I can tell you what they don't want. They don't want your pity. They can manufacture all they need all by themselves, thank you.

The same goes for your fears and dire predictions. They already have enough material to furnish Stephen King with horror stories for the next twenty years.

They don't want to be candidates for canonization. These people have enough pressure on them without being labeled "courageous," "brave," and "saints for going through what you're going through."

They don't want to be "left alone" to sort things out and deal with their problems. Never has their need for other people been greater.

One of the most unusual stories I heard about

friendship involved a cancer patient in Milwaukee who returned home after a bout with cancer and chemotherapy. He was apprehensive about how his friends and neighbors would handle his baldness.

He arrived home to a houseful of fifty relatives and friends who had shaved their heads so he wouldn't feel so alone.

Another incident of friendship involved a young camp counselor who found herself in the woods with two very small, very homesick boys who missed their mothers and were afraid of night noises. She suggested they both crawl in her sleeping bag where she hugged them and alleviated their fears. Toward morning the bag started to feel warm and very wet. Her reaction? "Isn't this great! They feel so at ease and safe with me that one of the boys didn't even bother to get up and go potty."

Okay, so you don't have to shave your head or tread water in a sleeping bag to prove your support for someone with cancer, but there are other ways.

You can be honest. Cancer patients recognize there are still some unfounded fears floating around out there about cancer being contagious. Tell them what your concerns are so you can deal with them together.

In one family, a young mother said, "The grandparents kept away. I felt angry and abandoned by them and all of our friends who had healthy children. They felt it would hurt us to look at their children. They felt guilty. My life was a mess. I decided if I didn't start educating my family and friends to the disease that I would lose them all.

"First, I got pamphlets and sent them to all the people I knew. After I broke the ice and they understood, they came around and started being supportive. I really believe people don't know how to react when a tragedy in any form happens. So they end up doing nothing for fear they might say something wrong.

"Everyone would ask, 'How is Travis?' Well," she continued, "I always wanted someone to ask, 'Sharon, how are you?' I think that a simple gesture as in a touch is important. To me, it meant so much if a person would put their hand on my back or touch my hand with theirs. To me, it meant no words can say what I am feeling, but I care so deeply and the touch was all I needed from them. No card would do as much."

Children especially don't know what to do about someone who looks a little different. They have never been faced with anything so serious before. They sometimes resort to cruelty. A young girl actually found it easier to tell people her limp was the result of a skiing accident rather than the result of chemotherapy.

It took me awhile. But I finally realized what my friend wanted from me. She wanted me simply to "be." To be someone to look at and remind her that I was what she had to get back to. I represented her life before it had been altered by her son's death.

I was the laughter she used to have . . . the zest for living she used to exude . . . the excitement for a future she felt she had at one time. I represented a "road of normalcy" that she had to find and reclaim, but she needed a beacon to light the way and lead her there.

That's what children with cancer need—some stability from their previous life that dangles before them like a reward or a prize at the end of their journey. They just want to see it, know that it's there, and get back to it.

Whether it's a "touch on the hand" that stirred Travis's mother . . . a simple offering of a tuna casserole . . . or an offer to babysit one afternoon, it's an expression that says "Let me help you carry your load."

For Heather, of Springfield, Virginia, who lost a leg to cancer, "the thing that meant the most to me and helped me to get through everything was having my friends come and see me. I discovered a lot of people don't know how to cope with someone who is different. They get nervous and do a lot of apologizing and smiling. At first, I tried to make them feel better and tell them it's no big deal, but after so many years and so many stares I now just make the people feel like crap and stare right back at them. I don't care anymore. I have my own life to lead and I realized I can't go around trying to make other people feel better about me.

"I got so many cards and letters that really

helped. One of them was from Sen. Edward M. Kennedy." She enclosed a copy of it.

Dear Heather:

I am so very sorry to hear you have had to undergo surgery similar to that of my own son, Teddy. I know this is a most difficult time for you and for all who love you and my thoughts and prayers are with you.

I am enclosing an article about Teddy in the hopes that it will bring you some encouragement. As you can see for yourself, Heather, Teddy is living a normal, active and satisfying life—a life which I pray will also be yours in time.

I want you always to remember that as great as a loss of a leg may be, it does not lessen the value of your life, or its value to those who love you. With God's help, I'm certain you will lead even a more fulfilling and purposeful life than you might have if you had both your legs.

With warm personal regards,
Edward M. Kennedy

As I scanned a copy of the treasured letter, my mind resurrected a picture in a newspaper from some years ago of young Teddy on a ski slope somewhere, and I wondered if he had found his way back to his "road of normalcy." Was it the smooth highway he had left, or was the road blocked with "rough spots of discrimination . . . detours of ignorance and insensitivity in need of repairs?"

I boarded a plane for Boston to find out.

10

Is There Life
After Cancer?

*People are taught we should look perfect. We see
all kinds of ads on television. I didn't think I'd
get a date in the world. I thought, "What girl
would want to go out with some kid with one
leg?"*

Ted Kennedy, Jr.
Boston, Massachusetts

He's called Ted now and he still looks like he
belongs on a ski slope. At twenty-six, he's tall,
tanned, and robust and occupies a small brownstone
apartment on a tree-lined street in Boston. His real
home is a sailboat in Boston Harbor.

At eleven o'clock, it's an early morning call for him, considering it's the day after the primary of his dad's reelection to the U.S. Senate, a race that young Ted managed.

When the young son of Joan Kennedy and the senator from Massachusetts lost a leg to cancer in November 1973, he joined an impressive statistic of the 40 to 90 percent of children who recover to live nearly normal lives. He has spent a part of those years fighting discrimination against the handicapped.

In an environment that turns out role models on a grand scale, survivors of cancer tend to stay in an arena that is safe and comfortable. They are reticent to return to the mainstream of the real world. The young man on the couch sipping tomato juice is the exception. He has resisted the courageous poster child syndrome. In fact, he's uncomfortable with it. "I come from a competitive family," he smiled. "After I lost my leg, I got on skis very quickly to keep up with the family. It was important for me to get on with my life and not feel sorry for myself.

"We're also a tight-knit family. They never allowed me to feel like I was different. If there was a football game being organized, they'd always say 'C'mon out.' And my cousins, they'd throw the football at me just as hard as they would anybody else.

"Believe me," he said running his hand through his hair, "I tried to use it to my advantage. When I was the quarterback and they were calling three Mississippi's and I was standing there, I'd kind of look 'em in the eye as they were coming in—there's that split second that you're looking for someone who's open—and I'd say 'Oh, aren't you big coming in and tackling some poor little kid with one leg!' "

They creamed him.

"I guess what I'm saying is I don't want to make my whole life out of my disability. Don't get me wrong. I'm very committed to what I'm doing except I want to do something else. I can still have a voice, but I've just decided I want to step down for awhile."

He posed an interesting question: How much do you owe cancer? How much do you have to give back? When do you stop paying homage to it?

Ted has paid his fair share of dues. He went through college at Wesleyan University in Connecticut "like a normal kid." A year after he got out of school, however, "my mailbox started filling up with these different requests to do these different things . . . speak at one place or another. I was approached a number of times by people who wanted to do a movie about my life story."

At first Ted resisted the offers, citing the invasion of his privacy, but eventually it came down to the fact that they were going to do it with or without his blessing, so he opted to work with them and maybe have a little more control.

His royalties from the "Teddy Kennedy Story" were treated as seeds to be planted and harvested into something that would benefit other cancer patients. Under Ted's guidance, they took root in establishing a new advocacy organization called Facing the Challenge. A civil rights office for people with disabilities was born.

"I worked initially in the field of employment and helped put together a network of people in Massachusetts who were currently hiring people with disabilities . . . all kinds. Then I'd go around and speak to businesses and whatnot about incorporating people. Most companies don't even have an affirmative action statement about people with disabilities.

"But instead of going around hammering away at, 'You should do this, you should do that,' I brought in other people with me . . . other businesses that had accommodated people, and they'd say, "Hey listen, I manage a hotel.' So that's how it originally got started.

"Slowly, it evolved into public policy and I'd work on legislation in Beacon Hill and Capitol Hill. About a year ago, I decided I couldn't do my work at Facing the Challenge and run Dad's reelection campaign, so I put it on hold."

Ted's work not only broke some new ground on the cancer survival aspect that is often ignored, but it focused on a host of inequities being pursued by other groups and coalitions today. Once a cancer patient is cured, a new battle emerges with virtually no support systems to help them.

Heading the laundry list of problems are: psychological readjustment, genetic damage, employment discrimination, the inability to get insurance coverage, inadequate access to good medical care, drained financial resources, and the loss of friends. It's like being invited to the party of your life and when you get there . . . finding out you're dressed wrong.

"We've grown up in a society that's in many ways sexist and in many ways racist," said Ted. "People have been taught and conditioned a certain way. The 'C' word. People don't want to deal with things like that.

"What you're basically going up against are tax-paying dollars being used to build inaccessible buildings and stuff like that. That gets me angry. I have always believed that it's not somebody's physical or mental condition that constitutes the biggest handicap or obstacle. It's society itself.

"The money that goes into research can help people years from now, but for the people that are going through it right now and have to live the rest of their lives without . . . what are we going to do about that? These people have to live today! The research is very good, but we can't lose the fact that there're people living now."

Ted is reluctant to look over his shoulder to sixteen years ago when cancer struck. However, his ready answers to familiar questions indicate he has thought long and hard about his disease and has come to grips with it.

Loss of friends? "People who never were your friends really to begin with."

Your 15 percent odds of surviving? "I thought I was immortal until I graduated from college," he grinned. "Kids don't sit around and say to themselves, 'Am I gonna die?' How many funerals has a ten-year-old been to?"

Concern for your future? "I just don't worry about things that, number one, I can't do anything about, and number two, the trivial things."

On becoming discouraged? "At first you say, 'Why the hell did this have to happen to me?' Later, when I was in the highest mortality ward of the hospital and I'd see those babies, I'd say to myself, 'How lucky I am.' "

Does humor help? "I was riding on the back of a friend's bicycle and we wiped out, hit a bump or something, and my foot was turned around backwards. I got up, twisted it around the right way, and walked off. The people standing there just couldn't believe it."

When I asked him about his future, he returned the question with a question of his own. "Do you have a crystal ball?"

Then he thought on it. "I don't think it's necessarily important to run for an elective office to make things work and to make a difference," he said. "I'm reminded of somebody like my Aunt Eunice [Eunice Shriver] who started a camp in her backyard that grew into the Special Olympics, the largest amateur sports program in the world. It's incredible. She has affected the lives of more people than any public servant ever has. I've got a lot of interests . . . for maritime marine policy . . . I'm very interested in what we're doing in our oceans." He paused and smiled broadly. "I'd like to think that the Ted Kennedy, Jr., story has yet to be told too."

He postponed his good-byes to whip out an album of pictures. When he found the right page, he was like a proud father. "Here she is," he said.

"She" is a forty-year-old, fifty-foot wooden yawl sailing vessel called *Glide* that awaits him in Boston Harbor.

As the pictures of his family flipped by like a home movie in slow motion, he brightened when he mentioned a visit that weekend with his ninety-eight-year-old grandmother, Rose Kennedy. He recalled how a few weeks earlier the family had sat around with her singing Irish songs. I sensed that his family, whose names had surfaced so often during our conversation, had been as instrumental in his cure as chemo.

On the way home, I thought about Ted's pictures and all the other family pictures I had seen . . . the cancer patient in the center . . . Mom and Dad hanging over their shoulders . . . a dog usually in the front row . . . and off to the side, a brother or a sister.

Every day of their lives, these siblings suit up for cancer. They go through the scrimmages and the emotional ups and downs during the season. They know all the plays. They are expected to be there. To do what? To sit on the sidelines . . . and watch.

11

"I Was There Too"

> *When Daniel came home from kindergarten one
> day, his mother announced excitedly, "Daniel,
> your sister is in remission." Daniel screamed,
> "Yea!" and ran outside on the porch to shout to
> a group of his friends, "My sister is in
> remission!" Joyously, everyone jumped up and
> down, clapped their hands and danced on the
> lawn until Daniel stopped and said soberly,
> "Momma, what's remission?"*

Imagine for a moment that you are eighteen
years old. It's a school night and you have just said
good-bye to your best friend, Amy, after gymnastics
practice.

You stand in front of your house and wonder

"Why is the house so dark? Why are both of my parents' cars gone? Why is there such a feeling of emptiness? Why isn't the porch light on?"

As you stand in the foyer, you hear sobbing coming from the den. Out of the shadows, a stranger approaches you. When he comes into the light you realize it isn't a stranger, it is Mr. Maguire, a very good friend of the family. He leads you to a sofa where he tells you gently that your brother is ill and has been taken to the hospital. He has leukemia.

You say to yourself, "Mark has leukemia! He is only ten years old. This can't really be happening. I feel like a lifeless rag doll wishing for someone to pick me up and reassure me that everything is going to be all right."

When Mr. Maguire finishes, he gives you a hug and a kiss on the cheek and sends you off to bed. Alone once again to cry . . . to imagine . . . to wait for the long night to pass.

After Lara Kain wrote her essay about that long night in Poquoson, Virginia, her mother, Marsha, added a postscript. It read: "It's important for other parents to realize how devastating it can be even if the brother or sister show no outward signs of their grief."

Actually, there are a lot of signs.

Younger children will sometimes develop physical symptoms similar to what their brother or sister had before they were diagnosed because if that's what got their siblings all the love and presents, it could work for them. If it was a sibling with a brain tumor who had headaches, they'll start getting headaches. If it's a child with leukemia who was just really tired, they'll be really tired all the time.

Sometimes they'll have regressive behavior. A kid who at the age of three or four was considered toilet trained will start having "accidents." They often have behavioral problems at school and their grades decline.

In the older age group, teenagers do a lot of acting up. They figure that negative attention is better than no attention at all, so they get in trouble just to get a reaction. If the only way they can get noticed is by being struck, they'd rather be struck than ignored.

Many children haven't lived long enough to develop the verbal skills to tell you what they're feeling, so they use only what they're good at—actions. But their emotions are real and the emotions have names.

One is called Fear: "When I was four I went to visit my brother in the hospital and he had patches all over him. He looked like E.T. and I was scared."

Another is called Resentment: "I'm not going to talk about my brother who has cancer—but myself, who like everyone else in this family has a piece of the killer inside one way or another. I'm a real independent person who, when confronted with a problem, likes to handle it in my own way . . . with only the Lord to help me."

Confusion is right up there: "For a long time I couldn't face going to the hospital to visit my brother. It hurt me to see him so sick. One day when we were alone I finally burst out after silence and forced small talk: 'I don't know what to say!' I'll never forget him looking at me and saying, 'You don't have to say anything, just be here.' "

Shame: "My sister was afraid to kiss and hug me at first. She thought she would get cancer too. But now that she knows she can't, we kiss and hug even more."

And the ever-popular Jealousy: "The hardest part about having a brother or sister with cancer is not getting attention, not getting toys, and not getting to eat in bed. The advice I would give to anyone with a brother or sister with cancer is to take it easy and be yourself."

Embarrassment: "Rarely mentioned but often lurking is another source of sibling guilt, humiliation at having a family member who is ill, disfigured, or dying, marking the family as 'different.' "

Apprehension: Asked if he had any fears or nightmares, Bobby said, "That my legs will get cut off also. I think about it a lot. I wake up and go into the kitchen. All the time I worry about it."

I remember one little boy who said, "Sometimes when my brother was barfing, I went into the closet and shut the door and didn't listen. It scared me so."

When asked if he had told anyone about it, he looked surprised and said no.

There are a lot of mourners and frightened people in the closets out there . . . young people who show up every day for the next installment of cancer. Unlike parents, doctors, and counselors, they have no active role to play in the disease. They just try to fit in wherever they are needed. But they feel. God help them, they feel.

Traci A. Maass, a fifteen-year-old from Arlington, Wisconsin, wrote:

"I would like to add this small story of a young boy with cancer to the book. He is being left nameless because I want people to read this and possibly put themselves in my place. If you feel his name should be used, then write me and let me know. No one knows I have written this eccept [sic] for my aunt and she isn't telling anyone. One day I will get up the courage to tell my parents, but not just yet.

"I remember the day he was born, like it was yesterday. I was only four years old at the time. I went and visited my mom and him when he was born. From that day, he became one of the most important people in my life.

"When my brother was two years old, it was found that he had cancer in his kidney. After the surgery, we had a period of time that no cancer was found in him. We were all overjoyed. We all thought that finally, together, we had overcome this and we were strong for it. But it wasn't the end. We found out, at one of the checkups, that cancer had spread to his lungs.

"I remember the times we went to the hospital for his treatment. I hated that place and what it did to my parents. It put so much strain on them and I couldn't take it away. I wanted to, but how?

"My brother went to the UW hospital in Madison. I was scared of that place. We did this for a few years but nothing helped. There was no hope. I didn't even know it. My parents and brother knew, but no one told me. I found out from my brother. We were fooling around one night and I must have hurt him some because he said, 'Be careful, I'm going to die.' I'll never forget the words. My parents told me later. I told them I understood, but all I wanted to do is ask why? Why wasn't I told earlier and why did I find out from my brother? But I didn't. They already had problems. I didn't want to add to them.

"We took him to Florida as his last wish. A few weeks after we got back, he died. And that day I died some also. Well, I have accepted his death but I still can't talk about him without crying. While writing this I had to stop several times to dry my eyes. I have written mostly about the bad times, but there were a lot of good times.

"He taught me about life. He taught me to

love, no matter what, to accept things as they are and not to question them, and most importantly, that there is life after death. There are a lot of people who knew my brother and helped us a lot. I can't name them all but there is one person who deserves a lot, Dr. Dorothy Ganick. I want to thank you [her] and all the people who helped a little boy to live as long as he did."

I wrote to Traci to tell her I wanted to use her letter in the book and, though I didn't want to be too optimistic about my expectations, it was just possible that her secret would be a secret no more after it was published. She let her parents read her essay and permission was given to print it. Her brother's name was Christopher Paul.

Sometimes people have a way of making siblings feel invisible. As Emily, age twelve, of Richmond, Virginia, wrote: "It's not like I wasn't there. I was there alright. I wasn't the one with cancer, but I was still a victim. No one knew that I went through a lot too. No shots. No medicine. Just pain."

But life has a way of going on . . . and dragging you with it whether you want to go or not. How do you cope, living with all this uncertainty day in and day out? For a few answers, I'd like to introduce you to two young Olympic skaters you probably thought you knew pretty well from the Winter Olympics in Calgary in 1988.

What you might not know about them is how

cancer was and continues to be a part of their lives.

A Tale of Two Siblings

It is written somewhere that a plane never crashes when you are riding in first class; Miss America never sweats; Olympians never have shoelaces that become untied and generally lead charmed, perfect lives.

Or maybe that's what we tell ourselves.

The reality was reported in a small paragraph in *Life* magazine in March 1988:

"U.S. sprint star, Dan Jansen, 22, carrying a winning time into the back straightaway of the 1,000-meter race, inexplicably fell. Two days earlier, after receiving word that his older sister, Jane, had died of leukemia, he had crashed in the 500-meter."

Dan Jansen was predicted to bring home two gold medals in speed skating, but cancer in his family intervened, and on that cold day in February in Calgary, he became instead the most famous cancer sibling of all time. He shared his grief before a televised audience of two billion people. His pain was translated into twenty-five languages throughout the world.

The entire Jansen family—all nine children of Geraldine and Harry Jansen—had lived with his married sister's cancer since she was diagnosed in

January 1987. "We were shocked and a bit ignorant, but we accepted it because Jane helped us."

As the Olympic competition came closer, Dan was torn between going to Calgary and staying at home in West Allis, Wisconsin, with his family. Jane was having problems with her liver due to chemo. She assured him, "Don't worry about me. See you in March." Dan was optimistic.

But on the day before the event, his dad was called home from Calgary because her condition worsened. Dan again felt he should return home but "Jane wouldn't have wanted that. She'd have wanted me to race."

In the small hours of the day of the race, he talked on the phone with the young mother. She was too weak to answer back. Later that morning, Jane died.

At 6:07 that evening, Dan stepped on the ice. "It brought to mind how when you skate you really have to concentrate. I never realized how much I took it for granted, but I just couldn't focus. They didn't even feel like my skates. My body was in Calgary, but my mind was in West Allis."

Families in crisis instinctively close ranks when one of them leaves a void, and Dan felt deeply that he was not there to make the chain stronger. "After I fell the first time I was disappointed," he said, "but I didn't care that much. It's so weird. All these years for that moment . . . a race I had dreamed of since I was four years old. Believe me, some things are more important than gold medals. No one should take anything for granted."

On that evening when Dan stepped on the ice, a more-than-interested spectator watched him from the stands of the Olympic Oval indoor speed-skating rink. It was his longtime friend and Olympic gold medal hopeful, Bonnie Blair. She and "DJ" had been friends "since we were born."

Bonnie was anxious for him. She knew what had happened and tried to stay away during the day so she wouldn't remind him.

"I watched him step on the ice and was concerned with his warm-up but figured he could shake it off and win. When he fell, I cried my eyes out. When he fell in the second race, I figured the three worst things that could have happened to him . . . did."

Of all the people who watched Dan Jansen that day, Bonnie came the closest to knowing how he felt. In February 1987, she was competing in Europe when one of her sisters called. (Bonnie is the youngest of six Blairs, children of Charlie and Eleanor Blair, Champaign, Illinois.) Since it was close to her birthday, she figured they wanted to wish her a happy one.

Her brother, Rob, got on the phone and confided, "Bonnie, I'm sick. I had a seizure two and half weeks ago and had to have some tests for a brain tumor." When Bonnie began to cry, he told her of how the paramedics arrived when he had the seizure and asked him who the president of the United States was. The only name he could think of was Grover Cleveland because he and Bonnie shared the same birthday. He knew that wasn't right, so he said he didn't know. They had a laugh and she even forgave him for not calling her the minute he knew.

As with most siblings, she felt utterly helpless. "Why him?" She said, "I had a feeling that when I saw him he would be changed. I wondered if I would ever talk to him again. My best girlfriend in high school died of leukemia and it hit me hard.

"I guess I've always had a philosophy—don't worry until you have to—our whole family feels that way. We're very close."

In April, Rob found from a biopsy that he had a low-grade, slow-growing tumor that didn't seem to be going anywhere; it was just there. Things settled down a bit until New Year's Eve—two months before the Olympics—when Bonnie's father was diagnosed as having lung cancer. Another decision was made by the family to hold off telling Bonnie until they had a full story to tell her. Nothing could be accomplished by alarming her with the competition so close at hand.

When they found radiation was a viable treatment, they told Bonnie. "I've learned from Rob and my dad that you have to live life to its fullest. I try to see the positive in everything. That's the way I've been taught."

On February 23, it was Bonnie's turn to take to

the ice. In the stands cheering the speed skater on were twenty-five members of the Blair clan, including her brother Rob and her father.

"Luckily, concentration is not big in what I do," said Bonnie modestly. Whatever was required, she had enough of it to win the gold medal in the 500-meter, the bronze in the 1,000-meter, and fourth place in the 1,500-meter.

In the stands cheering her on was her close friend and fellow U.S. Olympic team member, "DJ" Jansen.

Dan and Bonnie are world-class champions. (Dan went on to win the World Cup in Norway and Germany.) They lead public lives. But they would be the first to tell you that the real champions live quiet lives in West Allis, Wisconsin, and Champaign, Illinois.

12

Don't Forget to Write

"A breast or a leg?"

> *Question asked by camp cook
> serving food to a counselor who
> had lost a leg to cancer.*

As an adult, I cannot be trusted to write the chapter on "camp." I don't bring the innocence and giddiness to it that it deserves. Kids lie on a two-inch mattress and smell pine cones and campfires. I smell bug spray and mildew. They look at things that crawl in the night and see "bait." I see things that burrow under my skin and require major surgery.

When night falls, their imaginations come alive as they issue licenses to other campers to "hunt snipe." You can calculate my age by my height and multiplying it by the number of times I go to the bathroom during the night.

A kid's idea of roughing it is cooking pancakes on rocks. My idea of primitive camping is a TV set that doesn't bring in "Wheel of Fortune." That is not to say there aren't adults who are comfortable in Never-Never Land. There are scores of camp directors, nurses, counselors, and doctors who staff these camps for cancer kids, siblings, and families throughout the year.

They could write their own books. There was the director who had a herd of cows that discovered the archery range and ate all the targets. There was the mother who was apprehensive about being separated from her sick child for the first time. Just as she was softening, a counselor interrupted with the news that one of the children had slipped in the mud, dislocated her knee, and needed a stretcher.

These adults are there because they want to be and they're there because they realize camp has become as important in the battle against cancer as some of the treatments. They see firsthand what time away from the daily battle for survival can do. That is enough to sustain them.

On the flip side, they are the first to admit this job rewards them in a way few jobs ever can. I saw the children who looked at these adults with an excitement reserved only for a Madonna concert ticket. Kids who depended on them for rescue from endless days of being sick. Kids who had lost their places in the real world. Children who for a week or two each summer were given permission to be like any other kid in the world.

Camp has written a very important chapter about cancer. Kids get a second chance at the childhood they thought they had lost. Camp confirms the fact that you can put children in an adult situation in an adult world and give them adult problems— but you cannot take the child out of them.

If they only have one leg, they will jump into a puddle of water with it. If they pass a mirror reflecting their bald head, they will stick out their tongue in defiance. If you put 'em in a wheelchair, they'll find another one to race.

While you are reading this, there are two important things to remember. The first oncology camps did not appear on the American scene in any numbers until 1982. Why? Because before that time there wouldn't have been a significant number of children to go there—the successful treatment of children's cancer has been that dramatic and that recent.

Also keep in mind this is the only place a child can go and be totally himself. He is among friends who have shared everything he has gone through— and more. He can lay bare his head and his feelings . . . and not be judged.

It's an old camper's law (No. 192): "You will have more fun at camp if you maintain an age of twelve or less."

These then are the voices of people that camp was created for.

Dear Camp Sunshine:
   I'd like to get right to the point. The best part about camp was missing the last three days of school and my exams.

> Jess, age thirteen,
> Atlanta, Georgia

We got four bungy cords and tied Molly to a tree.

> Becky,
> Camp Ukandu
> Vancouver, Washington

CAMP JOKE:
   Q: What happened to the Indian who drank twenty gallons of tea?
   A: He drowned in his tea pee!

> Camp Kyso,
> Carrollton, Kentucky

"Sleeping Under the Stars Ensures Rain."

> Camper's Law No. 976

Dear Mom and Dad:
I sure do miss you, but I don't want to come home.

> Name withheld for discretion
> Nashville, Tennessee

I dream about the mountains,
Looking at the sky,
But here I am in my room,
Right by their side.
Now that I'm in the mountains,
I feel so fresh and clean,
Even though I haven't bathed,
In more than a week.

> Sandy,
> Madera, California

RUMOR MILL:
Frankie and Annette seem to be making a comeback. Could this be the hottest romance since Romeo and Juliet?

Going to camp was an adventure for me. It's the first time I ever saw a tent close up. In fact, it was also the farthest away from a shopping center I'd ever been in my life."

Beverly,
Camp Sunshine,
Atlanta, Georgia

Food at camp,
Was fit for a tramp,
With green eggs and ham,
I'd rather have Spam,
I didn't want to eat, but I knew I should,
For the food that morning turned out to be
    good.

John, age fourteen,
Bend, Oregon

"If You Think You Saw a Mouse . . . You Did!"

Camper's Law No. 1

Dr. Ritchey is a great Frisbee player. Why do you think he wants to be a doctor?

> Donnie,
> Camp Winaca,
> Morgantown, West Virginia

Two camp counselors were making tents rainproof one night and had an "interesting" conversation on love. To their horror they saw a foot sticking out of one of the tents. They were saved mortification when they discovered they were "overheard" only by a prosthesis.

> Name of camp on request

CAMP JOKE:

Q: What does a mother ghost say to her child when they get into the car?

A: Fasten your sheet belt!

"Clothes That Have Name Tags Sewed in Them Are Never Lost."

> Camper's Law No. 28

Dear Lupe:

Can you PLEASE tell Mom in Spanish that I really am having fun. I take a bath every day and try not to eat a lot. Tell her she better not forget that I am leaving on Wednesday. Be sure you DON'T FORGET. Well, good-bye. I hope you all DON'T FORGET. PLEASE!!!"

Claudia,
San Antonio, Texas

Toilet paper is held in the highest regard above all my worldly possessions at camp . . . over my clay, my toothbrush, my last week's *Sports Illustrated.* I vow never to waste toilet paper again. Future generations will not have to endure the hardships that I once had.

Keith, counselor
Camp Sunrise, Arizona

"It Is Generally Easier to Ask Forgiveness Than Permission."

Camper's Law No. 1092

Camp is the only place I don't worry about cancer. I worry about mosquitoes.

Camper,
Path, Rhode Island

CAMP JOKE:

Joe: Yesterday, I came face to face with a lion.

Moe: Weren't you scared?

Joe: Nah, I just turned and walked past his cage.

CAMP DOCTOR: Susan, how do you feel?
SUSAN: With my hands.

Dear Mom and Dad:

Did you miss us? Send a Yes or a No card.

Derek, age six,
Camp Hobe, Utah

Frankie attended Camp Can-Do and upon his return home I took his film to be developed. I was quite surprised to see him wearing someone else's clothes in all the pictures. It seems he never found the second compartment in his suitcase.

> Camper's mother
> Marlton, New Jersey

"What did you bring to camp that you didn't use?"

"Tap shoes and a new pair of earrings."

> Sue

"Mrs. Anderson? Robin broke a leg on the trail. Could you please send up another one on a plane?"

> Call to mother from
> camp counselor

13

When Is a Good Time to Get Cancer?

> *"I can't die yet . . . I'm booked!"*
>
> George Burns

You're in the soufflé of your life and someone slams a door!

You shout "Why me?" and then you whisper "Why anybody else?"

It will come as a shock to no one that cancer isn't something you put on your "LIST OF THINGS TO DO TODAY." But the reaction is always the same: "Not now! This is a lousy time of my life to get cancer."

Timing.

Five days before Christmas, the Mould family had just finished decorating their Christmas tree in North Vancouver, British Columbia. An hour after the two brothers were in bed, Tommy came to the stairs for help. He couldn't breathe. By Christmas Eve, Tommy was in Ward 3B, diagnosed with non-Hodgkin's lymphoblastic lymphoma.

"I was active in ballet, tap, and jazz and in excellent condition. One afternoon I was riding my stationary bike and felt a lump in my right leg. It was rhabdomyosarcoma."

"1983 was an important year for me. I was beginning the fourth grade, living in a new home, going to a new school, and trying to get off to a good start with my teachers. Then I fell and hit my head on a school desk. I got headaches and threw up. I thought I had flu."

Pat of Manchester, Vermont, had major plans when cancer horned in on his life. He and his brother, Brendan, were going to Lake Placid to see the Winter Olympics. Giving in to a pain in his left knee, he went to a doctor who diagnosed it as osteogenic sarcoma. After his leg was amputated, Pat was not to be denied the Olympics. He created his own event out of his personal irony—climbing a summit called Dawson Pass in Glacier National Park. He made it to the top—crutches and all.

Cancer never comes at the right time. Whether you're in the eighth grade and destined to be the first chair clarinet player in the advanced band or the returning athlete who was the hope of the team who returned with only one leg, it's always "inconvenient."

With Monica Furst the summer was coming and she was engaged in a running battle with her mother, Kathleen McKim, on why she couldn't cut her waist-length hair.

A few weeks later, the summer plans and the length of her hair were both out of their control. The eleven-year-old from Phoenix, Arizona, was diagnosed with Ewing's sarcoma requiring surgery and chemo treatments.

"I didn't want to go on living," she said. "I only ate one banana a day. I figured, why eat when I was going to puke it up again? My weight went down to seventy pounds. My mother cried a lot. I blamed my doctor. Then I started to think about what I was doing. I felt sorry for myself. While I was puking one day I just made up my mind that I was going to live and go to high school and the prom."

In a world where people live to be seventy and eighty, Monica wanted to be a teenager. In a world where the drop-out rate in public schools is a national epidemic, she wanted to go to high school and to the prom.

Prom night. It has a magic ring to it. But for Aaron Asencio, Crestline, California, it was the ultimate bummer in timing.

His story begins on the night of his junior prom. That magical evening where your friends are so dressed up, you don't recognize them. The gross guys who always belched out loud are on their best behavior. Station wagons turn into limos, and proud parents record the fairy tale event on camera to remember the rest of your life.

As fifteen-year-old Aaron stood in front of the mirror, he barely recognized the tall figure looking back at him as he gave a final tug to his bow tie, adjusted the lapels of his white tuxedo, and smoothed his cummerbund. A closer glance revealed his neck was swollen, but he figured it was just a swollen gland that would go away.

He was ready to dance all night and he did.

Aaron missed graduation practice because he

felt lousy, but after graduation, his parents, Adrian and Jane Asencio, had a doctor take a look at his swollen gland.

In the quiet serenity of a hospital in Lake Arrowhead, his doctor said that since he "wasn't a female menstruating heavily, he was probably a male with leukemia."

The summer that Aaron had planned to relax and do as little as possible turned into a visit to Loma Linda University Medical Center, which he refers to facetiously as "Motel Hell." The doctor's suspicions were confirmed. Aaron had acute lymphocytic leukemia.

"I was never sick up until then," he laughed. "Not even a broken bone. Biggest thing was strep throat in the seventh grade and 'brother beatings.'"

"Went into remission at two weeks. I didn't know that much about cancer. Mom's best friend had it. I learned something, though. A friend of mine had throat cancer and couldn't talk and had to write notes. I learned you don't write a note and go into a bank with it," he giggled. "Makes 'em crazy."

If anyone deserves to scream, "Not now! Enough already!" it's Michelle Hawley, Tempe, Arizona.

Michelle had already climbed her mountain. She had paid her dues to cancer. When she was thirteen, the fastest runner in her junior high school, the president of her class at church, a member of the honors program at school, and a musician who played the piano and violin, she was diagnosed with acute lymphocytic leukemia.

After remission, she started to put her life together again. Then the following year she suffered a stroke leaving her with a slight limp and without the full use of a hand. Four years later, Michelle had knee surgery on her good knee to remove bone chips. But she still trusted life and set about to live it.

In her sophomore year at the University of Arizona in Tucson, life was good. She was functioning like a normal nineteen-year-old coed. Then, the cancer came back.

In terms of emotions, relapse is hard to explain.

It's worse than going to Disneyland . . . and discovering it's closed. It's more traumatic than expecting a new bicycle for Christmas . . . and getting underwear. It's been compared to climbing a mountain and discovering the "real" peak is another two miles, straight up.

Actually, relapse is impossible to describe—unless you've been there.

When forced into a second battle with the disease, it is not unusual for children to consider suicide. Relapse patients mention the word often. Do not think that what you are about to read is a sign of weakness. You are looking despair in the face. You are meeting people who thought they were

going home and are being sent back into combat—
one more time.

These are the voices of nineteen-year-old Michelle Hawley and her mother, Sharon. They were interviewed separately. Their feelings were difficult for them to resurrect and sometimes painful to share.

> MICHELLE: Well, actually this sounds really awful, but when they said it [cancer] had come back, I said I wanted to die. I said, "Forget it. I don't want to do it ever again. Forget all this chemotherapy. Forget all this being sick. I'd just rather die." So, that's what I said.

> SHARON: She was very calm through all of it. She just absolutely refused [treatment]. She said she had friends who had gone through the treatment and relapsed and gone through the treatment again and they die anyway so what's the use of doing it. I excused myself from the room and walked down the hall and into a little room and cried my eyes out. I called my husband and said, "You've got to come. You've got to come."

> MICHELLE: They called my dad and brother in Phoenix to come to Tucson. They got a room for us . . . just to talk and stuff.

SHARON: The doctor and the social worker explained it to Michelle and she was very firm. "I won't do it." We talked about the ramifications if she didn't, how quickly the disease would take her, and the answer was two weeks to two months. And at that time I'm thinking, "My God! She'll be gone by Christmas."

MICHELLE: I guess my reaction wasn't normal. Because everybody, all the kids at camp, I guess everybody, if anything's happening wrong, you just want to get better, try to make everything better.

SHARON: Michelle maintained her coolness. I couldn't believe how stubborn she was, but I understand her rights. The three of us [her father and brother] were bawling, begging, and pleading. We just told her how much we loved her and how much we wanted her to live and not give up, please at least try, even though it was unpleasant. After an hour . . . or an hour and a half . . . forty-five minutes, however long . . . she finally said, "Okay, I will do it."

MICHELLE: I remember my brother saying—I can't tell you this without crying. . . . He said, "If you're gonna come back home, if you're gonna be in the next room just dying, I don't want to be there." And he said something like, "Since I'm your brother, I will, but I'm not gonna like it." That's why I love my brother most.

The Hawley family would never in their lives have imagined such a dialogue taking place. They were a family who should have been immortalized on a Norman Rockwell cover, a family who had relatively little drama in their lives. They're a quiet Mormon family with deep roots in their faith, who, according to Sharon, "had always had a great respect and love of life."

I visited with Monica Furst last year in a Los Angeles suburb where she is living with her father, Brad Furst. She was well, happy, and about to enter her freshman year of high school on her march to the prom.

Aaron Asencio had a day off from his summer job renting out rowboats on Lake Gregory. The next fall he would enter his junior year at Rim Of The World High School. I commiserated with the cheerleaders who, by the time they spelled all of that out, the game would be over. He laughed, "It was named by some suicidal, crazed maniac because the school is on the edge of the earth and just sorta drops off."

Aaron is looking forward to another prom night at Rim Of The World High School.

I caught up with Michelle at a Sunrise Summer Fun Day Camp in Phoenix where she volunteered as a counselor. She had been in remission for nine months. As she guided a couple of her charges out to swim in the 116 degree heat, her mother said, "I think she's done really quite well as 'up' as she is. I couldn't do that if I were a kid that age. She's a gutsy kid. I consider this a war that Michelle can win again."

The pretty young counselor did not die "by Christmas" in 1987. At Christmastime in 1988, I received a home-baked gingerbread house from Michelle and Sharon. They had made and distributed more than seventy of them for the holidays.

14

The Other Murphy's Law

When a patient says "Doctor, you can't possibly understand," I can honestly reply, "Yes, I do."
                                     Dr. Martin J. Murphy, Jr.

This book has made me "odds" crazy. Tooling down Kettering Boulevard in a rental car, I had to ask myself: "What are the odds of an important cancer research lab flourishing between a beauty shop and a McDonald's on a stretch of road in Kettering, Ohio? What are the odds of finding a parking space right in front of the door? Or finding the doctor in his office on a Saturday morning?"

If we're talking about the Hipple Cancer Research Center and its director, Dr. Martin J. Murphy, Jr., BINGO! All three turned out to be wagers that paid off.

As I tapped on the glass door for attention, I tried to remember my last meeting with Dr. Murphy. It was a brief encounter. We shared the same dais at a function honoring Daytonians for their contributions to life. His introduction was preceded by a litany of his degrees and honors ending with his scientific breakthrough of cloning cancer cells. Not only did I sit there that night feeling like a shut-in, I wanted to excuse myself and escape to another country. He was an act you don't want to follow.

Actually, I had come to the lab to interview two Murphys. The first is Dr. Martin Murphy, cancer scientist. The second is Marty Murphy, cancer patient. They occupy the same body.

I was not surprised when the white-coated Dr. Martin Murphy answered the door. It's a role he's comfortable in. He smiled broadly as he guided me through his facilities with the excitement of a small boy dragging his mother around a toy store. "If you had visited here in 1975," he said excitedly, "you would have walked into a single lab of about six hundred square feet filled with apparatus and centrifuges and you'd have to sort of slide around like you would in a subway to get through the aisles. [Today, the lab occupies eighteen thousand square feet.] But we were abuzz with excitement because at that time a great turning point took place. Do you know how a scientist defines 'serendipity'? It's looking for a needle in a haystack and discovering the farmer's daughter. We discovered how to clone bad cells. Today, we can take a sample of that living human tumor outside of the body, place it in an artificial environment, have control over it. We can ask the cell functional questions such as 'Are you a cancer clone growing in a petri dish? Are you sensitive to adriamycin or cytoxan—the list goes on—or are you resistant to these drugs?' We can do this outside of the patient and not put them through all this experimenting as they get weaker and weaker and their time and energy runs out."

When I asked Marty Murphy to talk about that night in Florida in 1981 when he was diagnosed as having a carcinoid tumor in his abdomen, the perennial smile lessened somewhat.

"It's hard," he smiled, "but maybe it's good that it's hard."

To no one's surprise, he reacted to the news of his diagnosis exactly as any patient would react:

"I repeatedly asked the same questions, having forgotten I asked them. I went from 'I can handle it' and I was macho, macho in the sense I wanted to protect my wife and my children, so I held it all inside. This catastrophe is a family event and they had every right and need for recovery along with me to the extent that I'm going to recover and that I've got to do it as a family, not as a person—and it took awhile.

"For a long time it never occurred to me that I was the problem. It made me angry. 'What do you mean I'm the problem! Are you kidding? I'm a solver of problems, my friend.'

"I thought maybe God in His own mystical way was awakening me to something—that there are special flowers and some of them are children who happen to be mine [five of them] and my wonderful bride, Ann, who is also a boutonniere.

"For a long time I couldn't talk about it to anyone because I couldn't tell people what I didn't know myself. I didn't know, for example, what it felt like to confront mortality and to look at Brendon, my youngest, and think I might never see him graduate from grade school or see my daughters' weddings. But the 'humor is on me now' as the Irish say. The principle is that cancer is an intolerable disease and I'm mad as hell at it. And I have always been, but the fact is our children and our children's children will someday be not only free of cancer, but the fear of cancer.

"It's like the story of Moses when he came down from the mount bearing those pendulous tablets. There were a few of his followers who rushed up to him and said, 'Master, Master, what happened?' And he said with that stern Charlton Heston demeanor, 'There's good news and there's bad news. The good news is that I got Him down to ten. The bad news is that adultery stays in.'

"There's good news about cancer that's coming out of patients—patients living one day longer, one day at a time, confronting the reality of the disease. Doing research is good news. The bad news is that we've got to do it faster."

It's easy to understand what makes Marty Murphy fight his own private battle for survival, but what makes Dr. Martin Murphy, the scientist, run? How can he maintain this sense of urgency and passion about his research when he never sees the faces of his patients—only a long line of petri dishes and tissue in incubators? He smiled:

"In 1970, I was a mouse doctor, so to speak . . . cloning mouse cells in Australia. I was seventh-year post-doctoral living largely off my father and mother. I remember when I told my dad I was coming to the States to give some speeches; he said, 'Does that mean that you are for the first time in your thirty-one years of life gainfully employed?' So anyhow, St. Jude was the second speech on my schedule. That's where I met Dr. Pinkel, who is now head of pediatrics. I spent two intensive days with him when I called home from a motel and told Annie to pack the footlockers but label them for Memphis.

"I had never interfaced with patients before—let alone children. St. Jude didn't have the huge building, that big hospital, then. It had seven beds. All the children were treated as outpatients. They were in waiting rooms with IV drips, in their mother's or father's or grandparent's arms. It [cancer] was everywhere and also the retching was everywhere. You couldn't avoid it.

"Dr. Pinkel put my lab right next to one of these waiting rooms for leukemia patients. So I went to Don [Pinkel] and said, 'Don, you've come through on every one of your pledges'—and he's known for that; his word is his bond. I said, 'The one thing I didn't talk to you about was where my lab was going to be placed. I gotta have it moved because I'm dealing with all these little white and black mice and it's just no good for me to come in and out with these children here retching and God, Don, this is . . .'

"He looked at me and said, 'That's exactly where you ought to be.' I didn't see it. Took me months and months of time. I got resentment for that man. "What the hell is he doing to me? To these children? These patients? I'm a scientist. I'm not one of these clinicians. You take care of your patients, but I'm answering questions of the cell." Then all of a sudden it hit me. We're just people here with a commonality of mission. For the first time I realized that it really had to be a team; it had to be a partnership. Don said, 'You have had the opportunity to pursue science. Now you have a responsibility to prosecute science.' I was pursuing my own ambitions. I began, of course, to convert entirely to childhood cancer."

He was quiet for a moment before continuing:

"I had to get marrow every month from some

of those little tykes and they would scream and I made myself go there and tell them why. They deserved to know why this was happening. Their parents deserved to know why. You know how a child can scream and sustain that screaming to the point where I mean it hurt. Oh God, I remember this one little boy and the parents from east Tennessee . . . the real hill country. They were dirt rich in the sense they had their riches of dirt. They were also dirt poor in wordly goods, but they had such a love for this little boy. He was one of the early ones in total therapy, three in which chemotherapy and radiation was given, and as far as I know he's alive and probably has grandchildren by now.

"On that day I remember telling him that after five consecutive marrows this was likely going to be the last one if nothing nasty grew in the dish. He jumped up on my knee—this was this little backside that had been invaded repeatedly with these horrible needles to get this marrow—and he called me 'Superdoc' and he said, 'Superdoc, I hope I never see you again.' And he gave me the biggest, warmest hug. I loved him and I hope that I will never see him again."

As the morning approached noon, Dr. Murphy surveyed his laboratory and took a deep breath. I followed his gaze. We were standing in an arena of cancer rarely seen by cancer patients and yet, their future lives here. So does Marty Murphy's future. Their futures are kept alive in this cold laboratory—

and others like them throughout the world—in rows of tissue cultures in petri dishes; in the computers, incubators, and refrigerators; under the microscopes that line the counters; and on the blackboards with their foreign-looking equations.

I noted a plaque on his wall and smiled, remembering how one of the kids told me about Murphy's Medical Law: "The more boring and out-of-date the magazines are in the waiting room, the longer you have to wait for your scheduled appointment."

The plaque on the wall of Hipple Laboratory reads:

THIS DISEASE OF CANCER WILL BE BANISHED FROM LIFE BY CALM, UNHURRYING, PERSISTENT MEN AND WOMEN WORKING IN HOSPITALS AND LABORATORIES AND THE MOTIVE THAT WILL CONQUER CANCER WILL NOT BE PITY NOR HORROR. IT WILL BE THE CURIOSITY TO KNOW HOW AND WHY.

A couple of days into the New Year of 1989, my curiosity got the best of me. I called Marty Murphy to see how he was doing.

He laughed, "If I felt any better . . . I'd clone myself!"

15

Never Take a Pessimistic View—You'll Probably Be Wrong Anyway

"Better Mottoes" Association
Dayton, Ohio

I told you in the introduction to this book that I suspected I would not be the same person at the end as I was when I started writing it.

I got that part right.

Before I was invited to visit the world of cancer two and a half years ago I thought I knew children pretty well. I knew they had the strength to move sofas if so much as a cookie crumb fell behind one. I knew they had the dexterity to take the bell out of a ball in fifteen seconds. This, before they could even focus their eyes. I have always believed that an army of fifteen two-year-olds could bring any enemy power to its knees in less than a day.

But I never realized how resilient children are—how much physical pounding these small bodies can take and still come up smiling. Emotionally, they are like corks. Just when you think they are lost forever in the swirl of dark waters and rough seas, they surface to bob along innocently awaiting the next assault.

There were other surprises. Their instant maturity, for example. Ginger from Tampa, Florida, was told by the social worker she had leukemia. Ginger turned to her mother and said, "Mommy, you don't need to stay while we talk." The mother hid around the corner to listen to this bizarre conversation between the social worker and her four-year-old child.

In a modern society where "tough decisions" has almost become a cliche, one cannot help but be awed by Kara, Greenwich, Connecticut, who realized that a bone transplant would have involved subsequent operations to keep up with her growth and opted instead to have her left leg removed. Her family was so astonished at her calmness they asked

the doctor, "Do you think we should call a psychia-
trist for her? She isn't upset enough."

The twelve-year-old put all of her feelings into
her poetry, including her version of The Twelve
Days of Cancer (with apologies to all the milking
maidens, squawking geese, and nesting partridges):

> On the Twelfth Day of Cancer my doctor
>   gave to me,
> Twelve months of remission,
> Eleven frustrated doctors,
> Ten Ewing's tumors,
> Nine prosthetic limbs,
> Eight bald children,
> Seven pairs of crutches,
> Six amputees,
> Five joking nurses,
> Four fuzzy wigs,
> Three blood tests,
> Two rounds of chemo
> And a big needle for my arm.

There were other revelations. When I asked
the kids for three wishes they would like to have
fulfilled, I didn't dream there were so many six-
year-old boys who knew how to spell Lamborghini
or so many eight-year-old girls who wanted to meet
Tom Cruise with matrimony in mind.

But the biggest surprise was their humor. Most
of it at first seemed like the dark side of Mary Pop-

pins . . . but it worked for them. I have always set personal boundaries of what is funny and what is not. I have been quoted as saying, "There are just some things you don't poke fun at." I was wrong. Laughter rises out of tragedy when you need it the most and rewards you for your courage.

Without it, it would have been impossible to imagine how these children and their families could have endured their load.

The giddiness of a moment when fifteen-year-old Jessica, Burlington, Vermont, with a "below the knee" amputation, was playing soccer and not only the ball, but her prosthesis sailed through the air leaving "the tall, gorgeous, humorous person I am" convulsed on the floor with laughter.

Sometimes it was a situation that cried for perspective. Ryan was treated for neuroblastoma at age three with surgery and radiation. Eleven years later, he emerged with no health problems, but there was just one little glitch. He only perspires and blushes on one side of his body. Ryan may use less deodorant than the rest of us, but his sense of humor was left intact, as is evidenced by his artwork.

Betsy of Boston, Massachusetts, speaks of optimism and humor as her "caretakers" during her bout with cancer. It put the following experience in perspective. The seventeen-year-old entered a treatment room to receive her radiation therapy. Several people were already there so she dropped her gown

and prepared to get on with it. Upon questioning she found that the extra people in the room weren't medical students as she had assumed, but painters there to estimate the cost of repainting the room!

Worth noting is that the incident happened in 1965, and Betsy added, "I wish there had been organizations and opportunities available twenty-four years ago to allow me to share 'experiences' rather than 'memories.' "

These children have a unique approach to their life-threatening illness. Instead of looking backward, they look forward. I discovered that everything in their lives takes on a new importance and that nothing is taken for granted. Not a friendship . . . not a kindness . . . not even tomorrow. No deed goes unnoticed. A mother from Missouri put a notebook in her son Daniel's room with blank pages and everyone who came into his room to administer some service to him was asked to outline his hand and sign his name.

When Daniel left the hospital, he had a collection of forty-two hands—big hands, little hands, hands that mopped the room, hands that held the bowl when he threw up after anesthesia, hands that held a scalpel.

The longer I was involved in the lives of these children, the taller and more perceptive they became and the more I diminished in size and wisdom. How many times had I threatened my children with the horrors of the "real world." How often had I made the ultimate threat that one day they would grow up and have to face a harsh, cruel world with all of its responsibilities and burdens.

Cancer. You can't get any more real than that. And yet, no one had to tell them how to deal with it. To them, it was a detour . . . nine miles of bad road in their lives and they took it one day at a time. Did we ever know that? Or had we just forgotten it?

I had to look at them and question when I lost the child in me. When did I become so rigid that I couldn't shoot baskets with the kids because I had to clean out the refrigerator and change the baking soda?

When did I look at a new puppy and see only

puddles instead of something to love that would love me back?

Was it the day I traded a live Christmas tree that filled the air with pungency for a practical "fake" tree that revolved, played a Christmas carol, and snowed on itself?

And small things. How long it had been since I had looked at a piece of worthless broken glass and christened it a "diamond" because I had the power and the optimism to make something into anything I wanted it to be.

The joys of eating snow and burnt marshmallows, burying myself in leaves, saving gum that had been chewed, throwing rocks, getting feet wet, and kissing the dog had given way to greater expectations from life—none of which seemed to give the same joy as those had. Don't even think of asking me to close my eyes and hold out my hand for a surprise. Trust was one of the first things to go.

When did I start dissecting relationships and all of their ramifications instead of simply asking, "You want to be my friend?"

I could produce a litany of words about what these children have contributed to my life: hope, optimism, pride, perspective, compassion, and humility. But those are just words and sometimes, unless you can visualize something, they remain just words.

I remember the word "eternity" was just a word until Dorothy Parker described it as "a ham and two people." Then it took on new meaning.

Take "Hope." It's a word that is used often in this book, but what is it? What does it look like? Feel like? Smell like?

A group of kids who had cancer and their siblings were asked one day by a social worker to describe hope. They sat there like portraits.

Finally, she said, "Okay, let's imagine that 'Hope' is an animal. Now what does he look like?"

Slowly and thoughtfully they began to put together this mythical animal that had been such an important part of their lives.

"Hope is about two and a half feet tall."

"He is covered with fur and it's fluffy."

"And soft."

"Hope smiles a lot and has blue eyes and a short bottle brush tail that wags. It is the color of sunshine and happiness. One ear stands up and the other flops down."

"Hope giggles."

"When it talks, you're the only one who can hear it."

"Hope raises its voice sometimes. It has to talk louder than fear."

"Occasionally, Hope is shy and likes to hide."

"Sometimes you can coax it to come to you, but most of the time you have to be patient and wait. Then it will come to you."

"It has to sleep with you as it's too fragile to sleep outside."

"If you don't take good care of it . . . it can die."

"You musn't cling or hug it too much because then it will become too big . . . and it would control you."

"It's an animal you can't buy or cage. You have to keep looking till you find it."

"It will come to you only when you need it."

"Hope has offsprings like any other animal. They're called 'Hopelets.' You don't keep them. You share them with other people who need one."

To these kids, "Hope" came out looking suspiciously like a thirty-inch, sun-drenched rabbit.

I have my own version.

To me, the animal "Hope" is small. Sometimes it has two legs, sometimes not. Sometimes it has hair and sometimes it is bald. It can laugh and cry in the same breath. It doesn't have to talk. Its very presence is enough to change the course of your life.

It has a name. It is called a child fighting cancer.

List of Contributors

In the war against cancer, the following have served with distinction and have contributed immeasurably to this book:

Melody Abbott

Becky Adams
Tigard, OR

Cathy Adams
Indian Head Park, IL

Cassie Adkins

Edward Aguilar
San Antonio, TX

Joey Aiello

Matt Albrecht

Norman Albrecht

Tony Albrecht

Matt Aleksich

Sandy Alexander

Talli Allen

Sara Allison

Dr. Michael Amylon
Palo Alto, CA

Emily Anderson
Phoenix, AZ

Joy Anderson
Nebraska

Kathy Anderson
Phoenix, AZ

Melissa Angel

Poppy Ansel
Phoenix, AZ

Nicole Apicella
Oak Lawn, IL

Luis Arcelay
San Antonio, TX

Mary Armstrong
Phoenix, AZ

Aaron Asencio
Crestline, CA

Jane Asencio
Crestline, CA

Arian Ash
Orlando, FL

Dr. Avery Aten
Alpena, MI

Lori Atherley
Phoenix, AZ

Nikki Atton

Vickie Auger
Richmond, VT

Marilyn Baehl
Boonville, IN

Marlena Baehl
Boonville, IN

Michelle Bailey
Montgomery, AL

Lori Baizley
Richmond, ME

Jill Bakun
Stow, MA

Sandra Bakun
Stow, MA

Aaron Barefoot

Laura Barner

Hilary Barney
California

Barrone family
Las Vegas, NV

Randy Bartholomew
San Antonio, TX

Taylor Bartholomew
San Antonio, TX

Lara Bartizal

Natasha Bartizal

Vicki Basler

DeeJay Beck
Atlanta, GA

Jane Bemis
Boonville, IN

Mr. and Mrs. Joe Benson
Tuscaloosa, AL

Susan Benson
Tuscaloosa, AL

Rebecca Berry

Heather Berryhill
Thatcher, AZ

Marietta Berryhill
Thatcher, AZ

Erin Bertinetti
Nebraska

Linda Bieschke
Park Ridge, IL

Karen Bigger
Las Vegas, NV

Ryan Bigger
Las Vegas, NV

Beth Bittle
Sharpsburg, MD

Bonnie Blair
Champaign, IL

Aimee Blanchette
Westerly, RI

Corrie Bland

Angela Blank
Arlington, TX

Annabelle Bleza

Kerry Bloor

Brandy Bly

Timothy Boles
Cincinnati, OH

Shyanne Bolton

Matt Bombeck
Los Angeles, CA

Palacios Bonifacio

Douglas Bork
Des Moines, IA

Julia Ann Bork
Des Moines, IA

Lynn Bowen
Cape Charles, VA

Kimberly Boyd
Moran, KS

Sharon Boyle
Billings, MT

Kathleen Braza
Salt Lake City, UT

Emily Brehm
Cincinnati, OH

Jerome Brehm
Cincinnati, OH

Kelly Bridge
Phoenix, AZ

Dayna Brister

Thomas Brooks

Cheryl Brown
Schuylkill Haven, PA

Jennifer Brown
Sherwood, OR

Joy Brown
Schuylkill Haven, PA

Julie Brown

Kerrin Brown
Sherwood, OR

Sally Brown
Sherwood, OR

Susan Brummett
Cornville, AZ

Susan Bryant
Auckland, New Zealand

Trudy Buchofer
Hummelstown, PA

Alison Bullock
Falmouth, ME

Mandy Burnett
Charlotte, MI

Chris Byals
Cincinnati, OH

Marrett Bye

Frolyn Cabal

Jonathan Camacho
San Antonio, TX

Inez Campanella
Baton Rouge, LA

Davis and Sandra
  Carpenter

Sherry Carpenter

Jeannette Carvajal

Yvonne Castaneda
Carrizo Springs, TX

Juan Castillo
Boise, ID

Juanita Castillo
Boise, ID

Rafael Castro
Laredo, TX

Linda and Richard
  Causby

Martin Cedillo
Laredo, TX

Daniel Chapman
Sedalia, MO

Jeff Chapman
Sedalia, MO

Lisbeth Chapman
Sedalia, MO

Karin Elizabeth Chavez

Shirley Chavez

Chris Childres

Cindy Claud

Eric Clem
Spokane, WA

Brian Clot
Mesa, AZ

Margaret Clot
Mesa, AZ

Charles and Vicki Cole
Rupert, ID

Melodie Cole
Rupert, ID

Cathy Collins
St. Louis, MO

John Ramond Colunga

Cecelia Considine
El Cajon, CA

Levi Considine
El Cajon, CA

Chris Cook

G. Chris Cooper
Phoenix, AZ

Richele Cooper

Michele Corrao
Phoenix, AZ

Kristi Correa

Carol Cotten
Phoenix, AZ

Coral Cotten
San Rafael, CA

Mandy Courts

Lauren Cowell
Anaheim, CA

Michael Cowell
Anaheim, CA

Robby Cox and family

Sybil Cox
Vista, CA

Craig family
Scottsdale, AZ

Crystal Craven
Grass Valley, CA

Stacey Crawford

Sandy Criscoe

Thomas Crow

Marquesa Curry

Beverly Cusac

Brenda Daniel
Glidden, IA

Joe and Katie Daniel
Glidden, IA

Darla Davenport-Powell
Washington, D.C.

Zach Davis
Nebraska

Peter De Estrada

Chastity DeVane

Louise DeWald
Scottsdale, AZ

Anna Marie Decker
Douglas, AZ

Jeanne Allison Deckert
Middletown, CT

Steven Deckert
Middletown, CT

Antonio Delgado

Kelly Delk
Phoenix, AZ

Jason Delp

Judy Denney
Watertown, TN

Melissa Denney
Watertown, TN

Mary Deviny
Redmond, VA

Patrick Deviny
Redmond, VA

Kara DiGiovanna
Greenwich, CT

Kathleen DiGiovanna
Greenwich, CT

Jack diLustro

Michael diLustro

Linda Dickerson

Michele Dickerson

Paul Dickerson
Phoenix, AZ

Mellany Diffey

Joyce Downs
Henderson, KY

Wayne Downs
Henderson, KY

Wesley Downs
Henderson, KY

Heather Dulin
Sidney, OH

Linda Dulin
Sidney, OH

Lisa Dunbar
San Diego, CA

Dana Duncan
Spartanburg, SC

Shelly Duncan
Tempe, AZ

Howard and Nancy
   Duncan
Tempe, AZ

Troy Duncan
Tempe, AZ

Daniell Dyer

Jason Dziendziel

Tiffany Easley

Rachel Eckland
Abilene, TX

Sandi Eckland
Abilene, TX

Mande Egherman
Scottsdale, AZ

Brad Eickhoff
Cincinnati, OH

Colleen Elliott

Heather Elwell
Livermore Falls, ME

Vera Entwistle
Australia

Danile Ermer
Olean, NY

Joyce Ermer
Olean, NY

Rachel Espiritu
San Diego, CA

Rose Espiritu
San Diego, CA

Jody Eulberg
Phoenix, AZ

Scott Evans

Amy Ferguson
Cincinnati, OH

Jamala Ferguson

Robert Fick

Olga Figueroa

Andrea Findley

Mike Fioritto
Phoenix, AZ

Phil Firmin
Auckland, New Zealand

John Fite
Arnoldsville, GA

Julie Fite
Arnoldsville, GA

Lee Fite
Arnoldsville, GA

Mark Fite
Arnoldsville, GA

Kathy Fitzgibbons
Phoenix, AZ

Dana Fladhammer
Tempe, AZ

Jon Fladhammer
Tempe, AZ

Anita Flatt

Vickie Foerch

Angela Foley
Tucson, AZ

Murins Foley
Tucson, AZ

Tom Foley
Tucson, AZ

Jessica Ford
Burlington, VT

Kris Foti
Tucson, AZ

Dan Fouts
Bend, OR

Eric Franck

Vera Frazier
Cincinnati, OH

Erin Freeman

Adolf Fritz

Helen Fritz

Monica Furst
Los Angeles, CA

Connie Gallup
Lake Zurich, IL

James Gallup
Lake Zurich, IL

Brent Gammoth
Phoenix, AZ

Janice Garathie
Hillsboro, OR

Julie Garbacz

Keith Garbacz

Claudia Garcia
San Antonio, TX

Andrew Garivay
Fort Worth, TX

Kathy Garivay
Fort Worth, TX

Brandon Garrett

Janice Gauthier
Hillsboro, OR

Gabe Gere

Peter Gere

Treavor Gere

Carrie Girard
Williamstown, MA

Patricia Girard
Williamstown, MA

Allison Glynn

Monica Gonzalez
Laredo, TX

Elizabeth Good
Maine

Lyn Good
Maine

Josh Goode

Lawrence Gould
Casco, ME

Bobby Gray

Sandra Gray

Chris Greth

Emil Griffin

Bert Griffiths
Wallingford, CT

Debby Griffiths
Wallingford, CT

Kristin Groom
Atlanta, GA

Bill Grubman

Elisia Gutierrez

Bernadette Gwynne
Maple Shade, NE

Billie Sue Hall
Altoona, PA

Mark Hall
Altoona, PA

Mark Hammond

Donna Hammonds
Fayetteville, GA

Nathaniel Hammonds
Fayetteville, GA

Tracy Hance

Mary Harlow
Cape Charles, VA

Estelle Harriet
Cumberland, RI

René Hart
Elizabethtown, KY

Jayne Hartman
New Milford, NJ

DeeDee Hasenbuhler
El Paso, TX

Les Hauer
Mesa, AZ

Michelle Hawley
Tempe, AZ

Sharon Hawley
Tempe, AZ

Elaine Heidrich
Cincinnati, OH

Jimmy Heidrich
Cincinnati, OH

Mr. and Mrs. Billy
  Helman
Othello, WA

Patrick Helman
Othello, WA

Misti Henry-Marsh
Wallburg, NC

Renée Henry-Marsh
Wallburg, NC

Mike Hernandez

Christopher Higginson
Las Vegas, NV

Cindy Higginson
Las Vegas, NV

Janette Hobson

Stacy Hobson

Suzanne Hobson
Salt Lake City, UT

Bobby Holbrook
Wolburn, MA

Jeanne Holbrook
Wolburn, MA

Kiffany Holly

Bonnie Jean Holmes
Binghamton, NY

Dolly Holmes
Binghamton, NY

Pamela Holt
Phoenix, AZ

Irene Hong

Paulina Hong

Rosa Hong

Elizabeth Hooker
Evans, GA

Jessica Hopkins
Hailey, ID

Lisa Hornyak
Alpena, MI

Christine Hovey
Concord, VT

Brett Howey

Debbie Hughes
Kalamazoo, MI

Wes Hughes
Phoenix, AZ

John Hunt
Phoenix, AZ

Robby Huntley

John Hutchinson

Sean Ihm

Cindy Ingles
Portland, OR

Daniel Jackson

Karen Jacobson
Phoenix, AZ

Vicky Jahns
Cincinnati, OH

Brian Lee James
United Kingdom

Dan Jansen
West Allis, MI

Kristen Jarman

David Jenkins
Arlington, VA

Gloria Jenkins
Walterboro, SC

Ni 'Ger Jenkins
Walterboro, SC

Sonja Jenkins
Arlington, VA

Jason Jennings
Arlington, TX

Heather Johnson

Jackie Johnson

Michael Johnson

Anne Jones
Stokesdale, NC

Nanette Jones

Tamara Jones

Tonia Jonk
Somerset, WI

Betsy Jordan
Springfield, OH

David Jordan
Toledo, OH

Rosemary Jordan
Toledo, OH

Marianne Judd

Lara Kain
Poquoson, VA

Marsha Kain
Poquoson, VA

Mandie Kaminski
Elyria, OH

Bob Kane

Eva Kapiniaris

Tammy Kastre
Mesa, AZ

Cassie Keenan
Gainesville, FL

Allison Keller
Atlanta, GA

Claire Kelly
Colchester, VT

Patrick Kelly
Colchester, VT

Shawn Kelly

Senator Edward Kennedy
Boston, MA

Ted Kennedy, Jr.
Boston, MA

Chad Kerley

Michelle King
West Vancouver, B.C.

Shannon King

Carl Kluttz

Gregg Knight
Albion, MI

John Knight
Albion, MI

Michelle Koblosh
Killeen, TX

Russell Kohler
Detroit, MI

Margaret Kovaks
Tampa, FL

Barb Kraft
Fond du Lac, WI

Kristoffer Kraft
Fond du Lac, WI

Robert Kreinberg
Portland, OR

Sarah Kreinberg
Portland, OR

Jerry Kruck

Carol Kuhn
Las Vegas, NV

Larry Kuhn
Las Vegas, NV

Beth Kulcsar
Cleveland Heights, OH

Christopher Kulcsar
Cleveland Heights, OH

Michael Kulcsar, Jr.
Cleveland Heights, OH

Michael Kulcsar, Sr.
Cleveland Heights, OH

Sue Ann Kulcsar
Cleveland Heights, OH

Erin Kwiatkowski

Sharon LàRussa
Pinson, AL

Shirley LaRussa
Pinson, AL

Jennie Lamb
Coeur d'Alene, TX

Lisa Landano

Kelly Langdon and
    family
Phoenix, AZ

Barbara Larson
Litchfield Park, AZ

Eve Leary
Glendale, AZ

John Leedham
Mandan, ND

Paula Leedham
Mandan, ND

Anisa Lerum

Eliot Levy

Ginger Ley
Tampa, FL

Kristen Lilly
San Antonio, TX

Cindy Lindsten
Sacramento, CA

Erika Lindsten
Sacramento, CA

Damaris Linnekin
Chicago, IL

Carolyn Livermore
Yucaipa, CA

Donald London

Ticey Long
California

Mr. and Mrs. Manuel
  Lopez
Laredo, TX

Tracy Lorimer
Shawnigan Lake, B.C.

Cindy Love

Jason Love

Joyce Lowder
Omaha, NE

Elaine Lowell
Renton, WA

James Robert Lowell
Renton, WA

Deordie Lupo
Auckland, New Zealand

Graeme Lymbery
Victoria, B.C.

Randy Lynnworth

Christopher Maass
Arlington, WI

Traci Maass
Arlington, WI

Melissa Machado

Avery Magee
Ferndale, MI

Katrina Marcam

Chris Markel
Portland, OR

Joe Markel
Portland, OR

Kathy Markel
Portland, OR

William Markel
Portland, OR

Clarissa Marquez
Tucson, AZ

Bradley Marrs

Marie Marshall
Portland, OR

Jennifer Martin
Hawaii

Julia Ann Martin
Narragansett, RI

William Martin
Narragansett, RI

Amanda Dee Mathis

Samantha Maurmann

Terri Mauro
Dewitt, MI

Jennifer Maxwell

Athena Maynard
Tucson, AZ

Jim McBride
Cheney, WA

Vickie McBride
Cheney, WA

Allison McCormick
Canonsburg, PA

Cathie McCormick
Canonsburg, PA

Mark McCormick
Canonsburg, PA

Mike McCormick
Canonsburg, PA

Anthony McCree
Montgomery, AL

Jill McDonald
Canada

Kathleen McKim
Phoenix, AZ

Lisa McKinlay
Auckland, New Zealand

Janey McMahon
Spokane, WA

Janie Means
Dallas, TX

Daniel Meek
Leawood, KS

Dicki Meek
Leawood, KS

Mellor family
Phoenix, AZ

Jeremy Mentzer
Portland, ME

Susan Mentzer
Portland, ME

Fabian Meza

Paul Mezzanotte

Carly Mihalakis
San Luis Obispo, CA

Diana Mihalakis
San Luis Obispo, CA

Teri Miller
Norcross, GA

Tanyale Mitchell

Toni Marie Molina

Craig Molnar
Holmdel, NJ

Luis Morales

Chip Morgan
Louisville, KY

Julie Morgan
Louisville, KY

Laura Beth Morgan

Betsy Morris
Boston, MA

Amanda Morrison
Farmington, NM

Marianna Morrison
Farmington, NM

Mason Morrison
Farmington, NM

Summer Morton

Sam Mossuto

Mould family
North Vancouver, B.C.

Kristy Jo Mouw
Grand Rapids, MI

Betsy Mowell
West Hartford, CT

Christina Muehl
Blaine, MN

Mattie Muldron

Jane Munroe
Kirkwood, MO

Dr. Martin Murphy, Jr.
Kettering, OH

Brenda Murphy
Beaver Dam, WI

Katie Murphy
Beaver Dam, WI

Christine Murphy

Bryan Myers

Pearl Myhres
Bowser, B.C.

Linda Nagata

Jean Nallia
Las Vegas, NV

Minna Nathanson
Washington, D.C.

William Needleman

Christa Nelson
Portland, OR

Mike Nelson
Portland, OR

Sue Nelson

Ronnie Neuberg
Columbia, SC

Bo Neuhaus
Houston, TX

Laurence Neuhaus
Houston, TX

Lindsey Newell

Mary Newman
Cincinnati, OH

Sandy Newman
Cincinnati, OH

Diane Nichols
San Antonio, TX

Celinda Niggemeyer
Toledo, OH

Jason Niles
Maine

Eric Nilsen

Dan Nordstrom
Lincoln, NE

Karen O'Dowd
Rockford, MI

Pat O'Hara
Denver, CO

Sandy Olijnyk
Phoenix, AZ

Lisa Ondayog
Hawaii

Brandon O'Neal
St. Louis, MO

Karen Orton

Helen Otis
Phoenix, AZ

Mary Owens
Auckland, New Zealand

Brian Paciulan
Topsham, ME

Melissa Paciulan
Topsham, ME

Natalie Parreira

Wendy Patton
Lebanon, TN

Kurt Paulius
Indian Head Park, IL

Mary Paulius
Indian Head Park, IL

Pam Pease

Shelley Peck
La Mesa, CA

Vickie Peek
Phoenix, AZ

Juli Peeler

Dolli Peralta
Phoenix, AZ

Dixie Perkins
Moores Hill, IN

Joe Perkins
Moores Hill, IN

Harold Perkins
Moores Hill, IN

JoAnn Perrin
Australia

Arlene Peterson
Fargo, ND

David Peterson
Two Rivers, MI

Kathy Peterson
Two Rivers, WI

Shannon Peterson

Cindy Phillips
Phoenix, AZ

Lisa Pittman
Pleasant Grove, AL

Frances Pittman
Morganton, NC

Diane Pless
Rome, NY

Erin Pless
Rome, NY

Larry Pless
Rome, NY

Brian Polk

Susan Powell
Winnipeg, Canada

Betsy Presley
Seattle, WA

Dana Prezembel

Raymond Price
Savannah, GA

Sandra Priebe
Alpena, MI

Alexar Provo
Tampa, FL

Faye Pruitt
Magee, Mississippi

Keisha Pruitt
Magee, Mississippi

Joe Puerzer
Harrisburg, PA

Sandra Love Quay
Altoona, PA

Sheila Quay
Altoona, PA

Jeff Quelet
Gaithersburg, MD

Margie Quelet
Gaithersburg, MD

Janet Quiding
Portland, OR

Ken Raddle
Portland, OR

Mary Beth Raddle
Portland, OR

Sharon Raddle
Portland, OR

Allison Rainey
Dinwiddie, VA

Christi Rainey
Montpelier, VT

Judy Rainey
Dinwiddie, VA

Jean Rakkila
Tucson, AZ

Margaret Ramsey
Somerset, KY

Michelle Randolph

Becky Rasell

Emily Ratchford

Mr. and Mrs. David L.
   Raub
Austin, TX

Eric Raub
Austin, TX

Lenna Rauser
Lincoln Park, MI

Michael John Rauser
Lincoln Park, MI

Heather Ray
Springfield, VA

Debbie Redder
Phoenix, AZ

Kathy Redder
Phoenix, AZ

Monica Reed
Eagar, AZ

Kelly Reed
Atlanta, GA

Nell Reese

Bruce Reh
Mountain View, GA

Tracee Reineke

Derek Remington

Kara Remington

May and Gregg Remsing
Modesto, CA

Shammie Reynolds

Cathy Reynolds
El Paso, TX

Peter Rhee

Sarah Rice

Lisa Richardson

Heather Riggens

Riks family
Mountain View, CA

Mary Sue Rischar
Portage, MI

Sean Ihm Rischar
Portland, MI

Elsy Rivera
Lebanon, PA

David Lee Rivera

Samra Robbins
Birmingham, MI

Staci Robbins
Birmingham, MI

Judy Robertson

Katie Robertson

Kathryn Rodgers
Darien, CT

Danielle Rogers

Scotty Rohelier

Jennifer Rohloff

Adam Rose
Bend, OR

John Rose
Bend, OR

Becky Rosell
Vancouver, WA

Carrie Rosenstock
Virginia Beach, VA

Jason Rosenstock
Virginia Beach, VA

Leslie Rosenstock
Virginia Beach, VA

Sara Ross

Seymour Rothman
Toledo, OH

Angela Rowan

Carole Royer
Portage, MI

Lynne Royer
East Lansing, MI

Pam Royer
Portage, MI

Emily Rudnick
Richmond, VA

Sue Ruffner
Buffalo, NY

Tommy Ruffner
Buffalo, NY

Cory Rupley

Jennifer Rutkowski
Fort Wayne, IN

Todd Rutkowski
Fort Wayne, IN

Chris Ryals
Cincinnati, OH

Steven Salomon
Phoenix, AZ

Claire Schechter
Wilkes-Barre, PA

Gail Schechter
Wilkes-Barre, PA

P. J. Schneider
San Antonio, TX

Laura Schulte
Phoenix, AZ

Todd Seeley
Ajo, AZ

Kimberly Seymour

Bret Shablow

Bret Shaklar

Nicole Shapiro

Heather Sharee
Tucson, AZ

Lisa Shaver
Arizona

Dana Shepard
Denver, CO

Jeffrey Shepherd
Auckland, New Zealand

Lynn Shoff
Lemon Grove, CA

Nathaniel Shoff
Lemon Grove, CA

Joshua Shultz
Altoona, PA

Sharon Shumard
Chandler, AZ

Travis Shumard
Chandler, AZ

Joel Shutz

Shanda Simmons

Albert Sizemore
Phoenix, AZ

Jessica Skibste

Jim Skinner
Carlsbad, NM

Jean Skrincosky
Richmond, VA

Jerry Smalley

Allan Smith
Australia

Amanda Smith
Omaha, NE

Chad Smith

Harriet Smith
Burlington, VT

Jill Smith
Prince Rupert, B.C.

Latusha Smith

Sam Smith
Burlington, VT

Maureen Smithwick
San Diego, CA

Scott Smithwick
San Diego, CA

Stacey Smithwick
San Diego, CA

Erin Snellbaker
Fort Myers, FL

Klair Snellbaker
Fort Myers, FL

Cheryl Snyder
Roaring Spring, PA

Patricia Solek-Fritsche
Indianapolis, IN

Sally Sovilla
Cincinnati, OH

Sammy Sovilla
Cincinnati, OH

Lora Spangenberg
Boise, ID

Erin Sparks
San Antonio, TX

Leah Sparks
San Antonio, TX

Myra Sparks
San Antonio, TX

Sparks family
San Antonio, TX

Jessica St. John
Fort Kent, ME

Connie Steele
West Milton, OH

David Steele
West Milton, OH

Kurt Steenblock
Laguna Hills, CA

Steenblock family
Laguna Hills, CA

Scott Stein

Maria Stephan

Chris Stephens

Judy Steritz
Springfield, OH

Tracie Sterling

Melinda Stevens
BAFB, AR

Russ Stoll

Hank Stone

Daniel Streib
Morgantown, WV

Donnie Streib
Morgantown, WV

Susan Streib
Morgantown, WV

Jeremy Sturgill
Texas

James Sullivan

Stephanie Summerix
Alpena, MI

Georgia Summit
Fresno, OH

John Swain
Toluca Lake, CA

Betsy Sweet
Des Plains, IL

Carrie Szermeta
San Antonio, TX

Ronnie Szermeta
San Antonio, TX

T.L.C. group
Charlotte, NC

Melissa Tang
Phoenix, AZ

Stephanie Taylor

Chris Thiry
Hoffman Estates, IL

Julie Thiry
Hoffman Estates, IL

Tom Thiry
Hoffman Estates, IL

Ashlee Thompson

Casey Thompson

Jane Thorp
Hawaii

Gary Thurgood

Jacqueline Tillman
Oakland, CA

Jeremy Tingley

Jon Toki
Cincinnati, OH

Masaji Toki
Cincinnati, OH

Tae Toki
Cincinnati, OH

Ann Toles

Jim Topp
Coeur d'Alene, TX

Anita Tranter
Cincinnati, OH

Joni Tranter
Cincinnati, OH

Kelly Tranter
Cincinnati, OH

Kevin Tranter
Cincinnati, OH

Jason Tritz

Donna Marie Trudeau

Sandy Trudeau
Great Barrington, MA

Chance Turner and mom

Brigit Tuxen

Margo Tuxen

Pattie Uberti
Milford, CT

Richard Uberti
Milford, CT

Karl Uggla
Los Altos, CA

Abbie Uhl
Cincinnati, OH

Jason Urwin
Cornville, AZ

Krista Vadnais
Rutland, VT

Frankie Valenti
Marlton, NJ

Shelly Valenti
Marlton, NJ

Jonathan Vaughn
San Antonio, TX

Heather Vaughn
San Antonio, TX

Holly Vaughn

Yvonne Vela

Ruben Veliz
Del Rio, TX

Mary Beth Veno
Woburn, MA

Alfy Vince
Vancouver, B.C.

Nancy Vince
Vancouver, B.C.

Luis Vivas

Debra Wade
Alamagordo, NM

Lisa Wade
Alamagordo, NM

Jeanette Walker

Annie Walls

Preston Walls

Raylene Walls
Seattle, WA

Julie Walsh
Boston, MA

Erin Warbington
Portland, OR

William Warbington
Portland, OR

Gay Warner
San Antonio, TX

Rick Warner
Salt Lake City, UT

Wendy Waters
Mt. Morris, MI

Marilynn Weaver
Midland, TX

Susan Weber

Mark Weidman
Spokane, WA

Mary Weidman
Spokane, WA

Susan Weintraub
Beverly Hills, CA

Toney Welborn
Faxon, OK

Samuel Weldeman
Phoenix, AZ

Melissa Westphal
Bridgewater, IA

Liba Wheat
Tucson, AZ

LT Whetstone
Park Ridge, IL

Lexy Whimpey

Danny Whitley

Mark Wilkening

Jennifer Wilkinson

Elizabeth Wilson
Salem, OR

Ilie Wilt
Anna, OH

Rodney Woodall

Keith Woods
Tempe, AZ

Laurie Woodyard
Smyrna, GA

Vicki Woodyard
Smyrna, GA

Adam Worst
Newport News, VA

Beth Anne Worst
Newport News, VA

Darlene Yancey
Benson, AZ

Patricia Yancey
Benson, AZ

Robert Young

Lois Youngson
Vancouver, B.C.

Carrie Zaagsma

Shelly Zak

Shellie Zambrano

Whenever I told someone I was writing a new book, they would break into a smile and ask, "What's it about this time?"

When I said it was a book on children surviving cancer, the expression on their faces changed. Their eyes took on a look of pain. Their smiles disappeared and their lips formed a firm line. They looked at me with a pity usually reserved for a woman who had just lost her bank card. When I explained that it would reflect humor and optimism, the look changed again—this time to one usually reserved for a woman who had just lost her mind . . .

Humor and optimism had kept these kids in the mainstream of life. Perhaps laughing and believing in themselves was a major part of their survival. These were kids who had every intention of living long enough to go to Disneyland, drive their mothers crazy, live in bedrooms that should be condemned, go to the prom, eat pizza for breakfast, and grow old.

—Erma Bombeck,

in the *Introduction to*
I Want to Grow Hair, I Want to Grow Up,
I Want to Go to Boise

Books by Erma Bombeck

At Wit's End

"Just Wait Till You Have Children of Your Own!"

I Lost Everything in the Post-Natal Depression

The Grass Is Always Greener over the Septic Tank

If Life Is a Bowl of Cherries, What Am I Doing in the Pits?

Aunt Erma's Cope Book

Motherhood: The Second Oldest Profession

Family: The Ties that Bind . . . and Gag!

I Want to Grow Hair, I Want to Grow Up, I Want to Go to Boise